Broadcasting and Accountability

Caroline Heller

produced by
The British Film Institute
Educational Advisory Service

General Editor:
Edward Buscombe

British Film Institute
127 Charing Cross Road, London WC2H 0EA
1978

British broadcasting has long prided itself both on a tradition of public service and on its 'independence' from government. This publication seeks to examine the whole question of how far broadcasting is, and ought to be, accountable to the public it serves.

The author

Caroline Heller was formerly the Television Commission Officer for the Association of Cinematograph, Television and Allied Technicians, Secretary of the Standing Conference on Broadcasting and Research Fellow at the School for Advanced Urban Studies at Bristol University.

Contents

Acknowledgements

This monograph refers to research material collected during 1973 and 1974 for the Acton Society Trust, which commissioned and financed the work. Its support is warmly acknowledged. The Trust is not of course responsible for the conclusions or for any errors the study may contain.

I would like to thank the Chairman and Governors of the BBC, the former Chairman and Members of the IBA, senior staff members of both organisations and advisory committee members throughout the country who spared me time and courteously answered my questions. I enjoyed talking to them.

Since the IBA may be right in supposing that accountability is a concern 'largely that of a minority', special thanks are due to members of the Free Communications Group, the 76 Group, the Acton Society Trust, the Standing Conference on Broadcasting, The ACTT Television Commission, The Bow Group, The Labour Party Media Study Group, the Community Communications Group and all others in the small band who have succeeded in keeping the issue alive over the years.

Caroline Heller
July 1977

Introduction

The democratic system in any full sense we can only discuss and imagine . . .
Raymond Williams

The origin of this study lies in two separate and apparently unconnected incidents. The first was a desultory discovery made in the BBC Reference Library at The Langham in the summer of 1973. By qualifying as a student of broadcasting and paying a fee of 50p I had been allowed in to examine the early broadcasting documents which were at the time untidily housed in a small back room of the library. Amongst other things I had come to look for the 1925 Crawford Report,[1] a crucial examination of the original British Broadcasting Company which led to the creation of the public corporation BBC. When I finally located the document on a lower shelf, the discovery was in fact that the familiar phrase about Governors as 'trustees for the public interest' that I had taken for granted in coming to check its context was simply not there. What *was* there was a different version proposing that the public corporation should 'act as trustee for the *national* interest in broadcasting'. And the question this raised, leading ultimately to a longer investigation than I had ever intended, was whether this was a significant alteration, and if so, what was its implication? What is the difference, if any, between the public and the national interest in broadcasting?

The second incident, in the setting of one of those rather grand discussions of the social conscience of the broadcaster or some such topic, was a confrontation between Mrs Mary Whitehouse and the Chairman of the BBC Governors. What struck me forcibly at the time was not the substance of their discussion – though I believe Mrs Whitehouse won narrowly on points – but how she was treated by the broadcasting professionals present, and in particular the gaggle of upper management attending the Chairman, in a way that was both juvenile and highly offensive. Since at the least Mrs Whitehouse qualifies as someone with a serious interest in broadcasting and as representative of a considerable section of public opinion, the question this raised was how public servants relate – or should relate – to the publics they serve. I was reminded at the time of Tom Burns' splendid phrase about the 'countervailing postures of invidious hostility' that are often to be found in service occupations. In occupations which serve a large and absent public such as journalism and television, he says, 'the compensatory reaction against the service relationship appears to waver between a cultivated indifference and contemptuous dismissal.'[2] Just so. What is the relationship of the public servant to the public service, and even more important, to us who make up the public? And how is this relationship to be expressed?

So these were the starting points for an enquiry that eventually proved considerably more interesting than the semantic niggling and bad manners with which it had begun. As a function of national interest and public service the problem of accountability is undeniably complex, and the IBA are probably right in concluding in their evidence to the Annan Committee that it is the concern 'largely that of a minority'.[3] The questions it raises, however, are of undeniable public importance and are certainly not confined to broadcasting services. What is the nature of a public service that distinguishes it from other sorts of service? Is the original legislative objective of avoiding the abuses inherent in the profit motive adequate today when the range of public services is so wide and so varied?

Nationalisation involves public ownership, but not all publicly owned organisations are nationalised; many are controlled by local or municipal authorities. Nationalisation also involves public corporations as the organisational vehicle, but not all public corporations involve nationalisation in its accepted sense. Thus the White Fish Authority, the Arts Council, the IBA and the British Council are public corporations, but they do not operate nationalised industries . . . In fact there is absolutely no dividing line, but merely a continuum between the nationalised industries at one extreme, industries with a measure of government control or influence in the middle, and private enterprise at the other extreme.[4]

And what rights, if any, does the recipient of a public service possess? If public accountability is a matter of public right to intervene in the management of the services received it has been argued that we are heading for a Hobbesian state of anarchy and disruption. On the other side it is being claimed that the danger lies rather in the creation of large public service bureaucracies that are insulated from public or parliamentary scrutiny and effectively independent in their pursuit of organisational objectives and growth. Finally, and most important of all, how can the processes of social change and political evolution be structurally related to the central policies of public services so that these services can be adapted to meet new needs and priorities?

These are some of the questions that this short monograph will attempt to discuss, British broadcasting providing not only an exceptionally interesting series of particular problems but also, I think, lessons that have important implications for the whole of democratic society.

Notes

1.   *Report of the Broadcasting Committee,* HMSO Cmnd. 2599, 1925.
2.   Tom Burns, 'Public Service and Private World' in Paul Hamos (ed.), *The Sociological Review Monograph 13,* University of Keele, 1959.
3.   IBA evidence to the Committee on the Future of Broadcasting, 1974, p. 50.
4.   Introduction to Thomson and Humber, *The Nationalised Transport Industries,* Heinemann Educational Books, 1973.

1 Institutional Origins

The origins of British broadcasting organisation have been rather obscured in myth and self-congratulation. 'A new illustration of the singularly skilful manner in which the British race seems to develop the art of Government' was Lord Allen of Hurtwood's comment on the BBC in 1932.[1] This legacy of narcissism is still evident in the broadcasting organisations' own submissions to the most recent Government Committee of Inquiry; however, as a trade union study of broadcasting has more tartly observed, although the coexistence of private enterprise and public service may be regarded as a triumph of British compromise and constitutional subtlety:

> the best of British luck might be nearer the truth. Whatever the achievements of British television, when one examines the way in which its parent institutions have been assembled, one can only conclude that they are a hugely fortunate product of accident, precedent, personality, informal contact, official design, and a remarkable number of loose ends, particularly in the key matters of finance and accountability.[2]

As far as the myths are concerned, amongst the resilient misconceptions that still cloud the birth of the BBC in 1926 in its public corporation form is one endorsed by no less than Lord Reith himself. This sees the creation of the Corporation as a unique constitutional development: 'the institutionalisation of a governing board for the first time in British or any other national constitutional history'.[3] Another version sees the public corporation more generally as a British constitutional invention of the inter-war years, putatively fathered by Herbert Morrison. Neither of these propositions is quite correct, and to the extent that each tends to isolate the constitutional problems of broadcasting management from the historical context in which they were discussed, they can be positively misleading. To understand the ways in which the idea of accountability in particular was approached it is useful to explore the origins of the public corporation a little further.

Origins and Ideologies of the Public Corporation

There was not, even in 1926, anything new about an independent board to administer a national or local service of public importance. In the nineteenth century British administrative practice had seen the creation of numerous *ad hoc* bodies of different kinds with autonomous or semi-autonomous status to handle various services and utilities of concern to the general public.[4] Quasi-judicial commissions and tribunals such as the Poor

4

Law Commission (1834) and the Railway and Canal Commission (1888) were appointed to deal with matters of regulation, supervision and reorganisation. Public utility companies, set up to operate services such as gas, water and public transport, came under statutory regulation as early as 1840 and many were under full municipal control by the end of the century. In a few cases mixed enterprises, such as the Manchester Ship Canal Co. of 1891, were established jointly by municipal corporations and private stockholders; and representative trusts, the immediate ancestor of the public corporation, were established by statute to manage local undertakings with Boards of Management representative of users and/or local authorities. Examples include the Mersey Dock and Harbour Board of 1857, the Metropolitan Water Board of 1902 and the Clyde Navigation Trust of 1909.

It is true that many of these statutory authorities for special purposes had a rough passage and some failed to survive.[5] In the view of the historian H. R. G. Greaves 'the only noteworthy fact about them is that they failed and were absorbed by State departments under ministerial responsibility'.[6] It is evident, however, that by the time problems of broadcasting management were being considered in the twenties there was not only considerable experience of independent management of public services under various forms of statutory control, but also that what were in effect public corporations were already operating, the Port of London Authority and the Forestry Commission being the most obvious examples. The transformation of the radio manufacturers' 'British Broadcasting Company' into the 'British Broadcasting Corporation' in 1926 was thus following a well established pattern of British administrative practice and experiment.

This transformation now needs to be considered in the context of long-standing discussion about the principles embodied in these organisational forms. The discussion continues today. It has sometimes surfaced as an argument about efficiency versus democracy, sometimes as one of public interest versus private financial interest. At times it has been variously fought out in terms of state control versus individual liberty, the rights of majorities as against those of minorities, or of socialist principles versus practical success, but it is typified by the following two quotations. On one side is an argument quoted by the Webbs:

> Parliament is supreme; and we cannot be better governed than Parliament is willing to govern us. It is in vain for a body of subordinate functionaries to attempt to enforce . . . opinions which are repudiated by the Sovereign legislature.[7]

On the other side is the view that:

> Efficiency in management is what matters most . . . The essence of industrial administration is executive decision . . . We think that Ministers should be directly responsible for commercial operations and the employment of labour to the least possible extent, and that the financial side

of these operations should be kept separate from the State budget to the greatest possible extent. The great Departments of State are not organised for business administration.[8]

The fashion for the autonomous body has fluctuated as the debate has moved between these two poles of 'political' and 'technical' argument. The tendency of the nineteenth century has been described as a victory for the effective control of administration by elected representatives. On the other hand the need to control new public services on a large scale continued to stimulate the creation of independent bodies and encourage emphasis on the virtues of efficiency, enterprise and freedom. 'Even while the nineteenth century crop of statutory authorities for special purposes was being gathered in to the capacious barns of the central departments and local councils,' writes A. H. Hansen, 'a new crop was springing up.'[9] This striking dialectic is maintained in some of the strongest statements of support, contemporary with these developments, for the principles of democratic accountability through Parliament. The MacDonnell Commission on the Civil Service in 1914 expressed its grave apprehension about the absence of ministerial control and parliamentary supervision of public services provided by independent bodies.[10] These were echoed by the Haldane Committee in 1918: 'There should be no omission of those safeguards which ministerial responsibility to parliament alone provides.'[11] These views were reinforced by the Bridgman Committee on the Post Office as late as 1932. Opposing the transference of the Post Office to an independent corporation (an event that has now of course occurred), it stated roundly:

> We consider that the public have a right to the influence which parliamentary discussion and control alone can give . . .
> Even assuming that the total or partial transference of the communications service to an independent corporation were feasible, we are by no means satisfied that the management of the services in question by such a body would infallibly result in the disappearance of the defects to which we have alluded, while it might be withdrawn too much from the wholesome operation of public criticism. Overcentralisation, absence of initiative, lack of imagination and failure to give appropriate representation to technical functions are faults which are to be found in the sphere of private as well as Government administration.
> We are inclined to think . . . that in the long run the advantages of the power of parliamentary intervention outweigh its disadvantages.[12]

Given this persistent and weighty support for accountability to Parliament, how did the independent public corporation not only survive but flourish during the inter-war years? The difficulty of adapting rigid traditional forms of central and local government to new tasks was perhaps in itself sufficient to ensure that 'attempts would continue to be made to remove new public services from the grip of the old',[13] but it does not explain the success of this

6

particular organisational form. For that we must look to certain crucial ideological shifts in the political thinking of both right and left as they faced the realities of advanced capitalist society in the early part of the twentieth century. As the influential Conservative scholar A. V. Dicey noted as early as 1905 'every large business may become a monopoly, and . . . trades which are monopolies may wisely be brought under the management of the State.'[14] The development of the limited liability company and the creation of huge firms such as ICI and Unilever, coupled with the study of 'scientific management' as a subject in its own right, facilitated the distinction between ownership and management crucial to developing capitalism. In addition the technologies of large-scale operation and international communication were becoming more widely available: office equipment, international telephone and cable systems, assembly line production and rapid transport round the world. The progressive business attitude of the time is well expressed in Harold Macmillan's view that:

> The Socialist remedy . . . should be accepted where it is obvious that private enterprise has exhausted its social usefulness, or where the general welfare of the economy requires that certain basic industries need now to be conducted in the light of broader social considerations than the profit motive provides.[15]

To counterbalance the state ownership that might be the necessary concomitant of desirable size and monopoly, both Conservative and Liberal Parties emphasised the dangers of bureaucratic inefficiency and meddling. The state agency must have, it was claimed, freedom to operate in independent commercial style. In this context the autonomous public corporation gained support as the chosen instrument of capitalist development: 'clothed with the power of Government but possessed of the flexibility and initiative of private enterprise', as President Roosevelt was later to describe the Tennessee Valley Authority to the Senate.[16]

Paradoxically, an equally important source of support for the public corporation was derived from socialist theory, which had always regarded social ownership of the means of production as an essential step towards the redirection of surplus value from the owners of capital to the working class. There was, however, no agreement on the practical form in which this ownership should be organised. Fabian writers argued for public ownership of public resources, but had emphasised the virtues of local and municipal ownership as opposed to that of the State. The demands of the Independent Labour Party and the Trades Union Congress were chiefly concerned to reflect the particular interests of workers in major industrial unions. By the time the Labour Party Manifesto of 1918 sank these differences in a general endorsement of 'common ownership of the means of production and the best obtainable system of popular administration and control of each industry and service', in a curious way the force of the demand was already depleted, sapped by earlier ideological warfare against the government bureaucrats and remote state control, which were seen by many trade unionists as potentially more oppressive than private industry. 'The miners are just as opposed to . . . bureaucracy as the mine-owners are', the miners' representative said to the Sankey Commission in 1919.[17] Thus the Labour Movement as a whole, which had retained a surprising degree of empiricism on these questions of organisational form, was open to persuasion as to the virtues and efficiency of management by 'experts', so hopefully suggestive of both a grasp of new technologies and detachment from an owner's concern for profit. The issue was reformulated as a question of good administration or democratic administration, and resolved by general acclaim in favour of the first. It only remained for Herbert Morrison to declare that the public board 'must not only be allowed to enjoy responsibility, it must have responsibility thrust down its throat'.[18] The greater part of the Labour Movement both accepted 'capitalist nationalisation' in the shape of the public corporation as the best form of social ownership, and agreed that such a corporation must as a matter of principle be exempt from parliamentary supervision of its administration. 'It is no wonder', says D. N. Chester in his perceptive account of the development of the public corporation, 'that an institution which claims to give us the best should have such widespread support – and induce in some a degree of scepticism.'[19]

The Birth of Broadcasting: Regulation and Legislation

In spite of this ferment of ideological debate and discussion of forms of management, the first move to organise regular public radio broadcasts attracted little general attention or concern. 'Identical noises to all and sundry' was a contemporary description of broadcasting quoted by Asa Briggs in his history of the BBC.[20] It seemed to most people, including politicians, to be a matter of relatively minor technical operation in a commercial field of relatively little public importance. Except, that is, for the fact that the proposed activities intruded upon the jealously guarded sector of telecommunications which had always been centrally controlled as a matter vital to national security. For this reason alone the moves of enterprising radio manufacturers attracted the attention of vigilant Post Office officials. It was this accidental conjunction of state interest and commercial enterprise that led to the negotiations that finally produced the British Broadcasting Co. Ltd. in January 1923, with John Reith as its first General Manager. In 1926, after two extensive public inquiries into the technical and social problems of broadcasting management (under Sir Frederick Sykes in 1923 and the Earl of Crawford and Balcarres in 1925), the British Broadcasting Co. Ltd. was replaced by the British Broadcasting Corporation, created by Royal Charter. It is the Charter (together with the Licence and Agreement between the Post Office and the broadcasting authorities, which gives the necessary technical permission to transmit) that provides the basis of broadcasting regulation in this country. Although the creation of ITV represented a major upheaval in both the organisation and nature of broadcasting in the UK, in constitutional

8

terms the Television Act of 1954 reproduced in all essential respects the terms
on which radio services began in 1923.[21]

As the Committee of Inquiry under Lord Beveridge observed in its report in
1951:

> the formal power of the Government of the day over the BBC is absolute.
> The Governors who constitute the Corporation can be removed at any time
> by Order in Council and can be replaced by others. The Licence can be
> revoked by the PMG if at any time in his opinion it is failing in its duties. The
> PMG can veto any proposed broadcast or class of broadcast, and in doing so
> can require the Corporation to broadcast any announcement or other
> matter desired by it.[22]

However, 'in practice', the Committee went on:

> it has become the agreed policy of successive Governments, accepted by
> Parliament, that the Corporation should be independent of the
> Government of the day . . .

Reith's view of all this was succinct: 'An odd sort of muddle up' was how he
described it, and this is confirmed by Asa Briggs' marvellously detailed
accounts of the early discussions during the twenties. Although the BBC has
since been much quoted as a desirable model for the management of
nationalised enterprises, it was not established, in the opinion of D. N.
Chester, 'as any sort of thought out answer to the problems of management set
by nationalised industries'.[23] The whole question of monopoly, for example,
though discussed, was left *de facto* rather than *de jure*. Questions of finance
remained confused, to provide a constant source of friction throughout the
thirties and up to the present time. And accountability, the central matter of
the relationship of Parliament and people to a public service, was not
specifically considered at all.

Factors in the Organisation of Broadcasting Services

It was this system, which Reith described as being introduced 'while the
watchmen slept',[24] that has provided the framework of broadcasting
legislation and control which has lasted through the growth of television and
the introduction of commercial broadcasting up to the present day. In the
perspective of our current anxieties and discontents about control of public
services in general and of broadcasting policy in particular, it is interesting to
consider in retrospect some of the factors that shaped these remarkably
resilient instruments of broadcasting legislation fifty years ago.

The first lies in the nature of technological change, and in the complicated
ways by which technology can be described as responding to social needs and
also as shaping them. These have been brilliantly analysed by Raymond
Williams in the opening chapters of his book *Television: Technology and*

Cultural Form. At one level, he suggests, the development of modern communications technology can be seen as a direct response to the problems of communications and control in the military and commercial operations of expanded, mobile and complex societies. At another level, it is the changes produced by such developments that induce new interpretations of need which in turn stimulate further development. 'An increased awareness of mobility and change, not just as abstractions but as lived experiences, led to a major redefinition, in practice and then in theory, of the function and process of social communication . . .'[25] The needs that broadcasting developed to satisfy may be partly understood in terms of the newly defined and sanctioned leisure of the working classes which industrially organised amusement services were designed to fill, a subject on which Tom Burns has made perceptive comment.[26] But it is also significant that systems for the distribution and reception of radio, and later television, were devised as abstract processes without definition of the content that was to fill them. As Williams notes, 'It is not only that the supply of broadcasting facilities preceded demand; it is that the means of communication preceded their content.'[27] The organisation of broadcasting services was therefore in this special sense peripheral to perceived government or social purposes at the time, and was conceived outside them purely as a function of the marketing of radio equipment. In exactly the same way satellite and cable systems are now in search of social functions outside the military research that created their original technologies.

In terms of Williams' analysis the development of transmission and reception facilities created a demand from radio manufacturers for regular broadcasting services which would stimulate public awareness of the need for sets to receive them. This emphasis on general forms, rather than particular content, and the historical precedence of the techniques of delivery and reception over demand, may go some way to explain the remarkable absence of concern shown at the time for what was actually to be broadcast. The Crawford Committee suggested 'a moderate amount of controversial matter should be broadcast, provided it is of high quality and distributed with scrupulous fairness.'[28] The dominant assumption was that a consensus existed on what it was desirable for the public to hear. What was undesirable could be catalogued in negative prohibitions: it was necessary to avoid the vulgarities of American experience, to omit news in deference to press interests, to avoid (in the early days at least) controversial topics such as politics. Since the problem of fundamental disagreement about the content and purposes of broadcasting appeared academic, it is not surprising that issues of accountability did not figure in the arguments. There was of course a testing moment during the General Strike of 1926, just as the life of the British Broadcasting Company was coming to an end and the Crawford Committee was about to report on future structures of broadcasting. The threat of Government take over was averted by the obsequious posture of the Company (described by Reith with candour as 'an awkward one'[29]), in acceding to Government demands on programming. As he wrote later in his diary, 'they know that they can trust us not to be really impartial'.[30]

10

Broadcasting 'triumphantly showed itself in a searching test', Baldwin told Reith,[31] and given this assurance the emphasis of the time was neatly expressed by the National Association of Radio Manufacturers in evidence to the Sykes Committee when it explained that 'the interests of the manufacturers lie in the provision of efficient and ever improving quality of broadcasting'.[32]

It is as a corollary of this emergence of public broadcasting largely outside the spheres of central government activity that the second factor, the special relationship of broadcasting and the state, should be considered. A special relationship has always linked communications services with the economic and political purposes of the State in all countries. This is usually represented by the status of the Post Office as a government monopoly with control over what are regarded as vital technical services. In Britain the Telegraphy Acts of 1863, 1868, 1869 and a series of Wireless Telegraphy Acts since 1904 have formally consolidated state control of telecommunications. (It is often forgotten that Gladstone carried out the nationalisation of the telegraphy service with the 1869 Act.) As George Wedell has noted, Government interest in broadcasting (vested in the Postmaster General, later the Minister of Posts and Telecommunications, and most recently divided between the Secretary of State for Industry and the Home Secretary) derives, as it were, incidentally from these traditional technical concerns.[33] The State's interest in broadcasting is thus essentially negative, concerned to protect essential services from outside interference and disruption. This is expressed by its control of frequency allocation and the legal regulation (by licensing) of the right to transmit and receive messages. The positive matters of content and social purpose, on the other hand, were originally seen as peripheral, the Post Office being among the first to suggest that it would be inappropriate for it to 'accept responsibility or to defend the proceedings of the Corporation in Parliament'.[34]

There is no doubt that since then the social controversies increasingly involved in broadcasting policy have proved something of an embarrassment to this ordinarily rather workaday department. The office of Postmaster General (and later, the Minister of Posts and Telecommunications) has traditionally been regarded as a position for a politician moving rapidly either up or down (though the throughput of seven Postmasters General during the crucial '21–'24 period was more than usually rapid). The office has not carried much status within the hierarchy of Ministers, and broadcasting has therefore had to seek other more senior spokesmen to raise matters of policy at Cabinet level. The reorganisation of broadcasting responsibilities in 1974 belatedly recognises the social as well as technical implications of radio and television by separating out broadcasting policy and frequency allocation (under the Home Office) from Post Office matters and telecommunications issues (located at the Department of Trade and Industry). It remains to be seen whether this new machinery for handling broadcasting policy, a subject in which the technical development of communications systems is so closely intertwined with the character and impact of radio and television services, can provide a satisfactory basis for either negative or positive formulation of national requirements.

Another aspect of the technical base of the national interest in broadcasting as perceived in the twenties should be briefly mentioned. This is the part played in early discussions by the Wireless Sub-Committee of the influential Imperial Communications Committee. This body was an offshoot of the Imperial Defence Committee, representing the interests of the Armed Services as well as the Foreign Office, Colonial Office, Treasury, War Department and Board of Trade. It is no accident that the decisive technical restrictions imposed on the BBC in 1922 were derived from this Committee's recommendations.[35]

Two other factors of a rather different kind also played a part in the shaping of broadcasting legislation and institutions. One was the parallel experience of broadcasting in the United States. Throughout the history of radio and television in Britain, the American example has provided an immensely influential devil's advocacy of alternatives: hellfire accounts of chaos and tastelessness, stirring images of freedom, enterprise and imagination. Radio in the United States in the twenties was advancing rapidly on an unrestricted free enterprise basis. Peter Eckersley, a pioneer of British broadcasting, described the American experience as 'a great stimulant', and referred to the people who 'came over from the States and pointed out what vast sums of money were being made there'. On the other hand there is no doubt that it was the horrified reports of technical anarchy brought back from the States and relayed to Sykes, Crawford and the Imperial Communications Committee that helped to create a climate of opinion receptive to the public corporation monopoly dedicated to Reithian public service. The dominant concern of the State and the Corporation in these circumstances was not state control – indeed this was specifically rejected – but the elimination of the profit motive and any possibility of disorderly exploitation of public resources.

The other factor was of course Reith himself. Reith was wholly positive in his 'high conception of the inherent possibility of the service' and in his speedy assessment of the 'brute force of monopoly' essential to the maintenance of this vision. Equally significant was his recognition of the connection of the fashionable idea of efficiency with his goal of independent management. By the twenties even an old Guild Socialist like G. D. H. Cole had been persuaded that 'management was essentially an affair of experts to whom it was indispensable to give wide discretionary power and a liberal freedom in experiment with new methods.'[36] This was Reith's view of the matter exactly. 'Unencumbered, unembarrassed, and unconditional *efficiency*', he wrote in *The Times*, was the determining reason for turning the British Broadcasting Company into a public corporation. It could then, in his words, be:

> normally untrammelled by any political intereference, by any delegacy, by any Civil Service procedures, by any political party expectations and claims, by any demands, by any impatient shareholders – not one factor of the kind that disquiets the life of most administrators and managers.[37]

In one of the most interesting judgments of his study of the BBC, Asa Briggs concludes that it was the form and conduct of radio services under Reith at the British Broadcasting Company that decisively shaped the legislative approach to broadcasting's future. Contrary to general belief, it was the private enterprise company and not the Government that effectively put the seal of public service on broadcasting. The first Chairman of the new Corporation saw it as a 'logical and inevitable result'[38] of the policies adopted from the foundation of the Company in 1922. This was Reith's doing.

It is always difficult to assess the individual's contribution and Reith's may well have been overemphasised by popular myth and official hagiography. However, there is no doubt that his particular presence at a particular moment in the birth of broadcasting services in the UK was decisive. It was his natural awareness of the implicit political boundaries to his broadcasting domain, coupled with his unbounded confidence in his own private communication channels with the Almighty, that bridged the awkward gap between public services and State control. Without his unique combination of megalomania, subservience and administrative ability, the future of British broadcasting would have been different, and possibly very different. This is a not ignoble epitaph for a curious and very remarkable man.[39]

Considered in retrospect, the birth of broadcasting was an extraordinarily casual affair. However, it has to be remembered that these were services originated in response to commercial and technical initiatives rather than to popular demand or Government policy. The challenge presented by these initiatives was primarily to the existing state interest in telecommunications. This was resolved by legislation which retained for the State, as is still retained, absolute control over the technical aspects of broadcasting as well as its content. The model of the public corporation was conveniently to hand to provide precisely the safeguarding of Government concerns, protection from the profit motive and the independent pursuit of efficiency which were seen as necessary to the development of radio. (It is significant that these models were drawn from working examples dealing with relatively uncontroversial matters of public utility supply, and that the unhappy experiments with Poor Law Administration were forgotten.) As for disquiet about the social consequences of the new medium, what anxieties existed were allayed by Reith's zeal in dedicating radio to the cause of social uplift and improvement.[40] Who wished to argue, or indeed foresaw that anyone would ever wish to argue, with the goal of 'good broadcasting'?

In 1926, when public service broadcasting in its public corporation form began, it was seen as sufficient that the Crawford Committee had designated the Corporation as 'trustee for the national interest in broadcasting'.[41] The machinery of accountability was given no further attention quite simply because neither the potential of broadcasting nor the possibility of fundamental disagreement about its objectives had been considered. Both, however, have come to dominate the conduct and discussion of broadcasting services. How the broadcasting organisations themselves have responded to these disturbing realities is examined in the next chapter.

13

Notes

1. Lord Allen of Hurtwood, in a letter to Malcolm MacDonald, 1932. Quoted by Asa Briggs in *The History of Broadcasting in the UK*, OUP, 1965, Volume II: *The Golden Age of Wireless*, p. 420.
2. ACTT *Television Commission Report* to Annual Conference 1972, p. 16. A study of British television, and proposals for reform, prepared by the Association of Cinematograph, Television and Allied Technicians, 2 Soho Square, London W1.
3. Lord Reith, 'The Facade of Public Corporations', an article in *The Times*, March 29, 1966. Quoted by E. G. Wedell in *Broadcasting and Public Policy*, Michael Joseph, 1968, p. 21.
4. See Edward Goodman, *Forms of Public Control and Ownership,* Christophers, 1951, for an interesting account from which the examples in this section are drawn.
5. The Poor Law Commission, for example, which was ended in 1847.
6. H. R. G. Greaves, 'Public Boards and Corporations', *The Political Quarterly*, Vol. XVI No. 1, January 1945.
7. Letter from Sir George Cornewall Lewis to Grote, quoted in the Webbs' *English Poor Law History*, Part 2, Volume II, Longmans Green, 1929.
8. *Britain's Industrial Future*, a Liberal Party Report of 1929, quoted in A. H. Hanson (ed.), *Nationalisation, a Book of Readings*, George Allen and Unwin, 1963.
9. A. H. Hanson, *Parliamentary and Public Ownership*, Hansard Society, 1961, p. 15.
10. *Commission on the Civil Service, 1914* (Macdonnell Commission), Fourth Report. Quoted by A. H. Hanson in *Parliament and Public Ownership*, op. cit.
11. *Committee on the Machinery of Government 1918* (The Haldane Committee), HMSO Cmnd. 9230, p. 11.
12. *Report of the Committee of Inquiry on the Post Office 1932*, HMSO Cmnd. 4149.
13. H. R. G. Greaves, op. cit.
14. A. V. Dicey, *Lectures on the Relation between Law and Public Opinion in England during the 19th Century*, p. 248, quoted by Briggs, *The Golden Age of Wireless*, op. cit., p. 419.
15. Harold MacMillan, *The Middle Way*, MacMillan, 1938, p. 239, quoted by Thompson and Hunter, *The Nationalised Transport Industries*, Heinemann Educational Books, 1973, p. 9.
16. Quoted by Lincoln Gordon, *The Public Corporation in Great Britain*, OUP, 1937.
17. Miners Federation evidence to the Sankey Commission, 1919. Quoted by D. N. Chester in 'Management in the Nationalised Industries', *Public Administration*, Vol. XXX, Spring 1952.
18. Herbert Morrison, *Socialisation and Transport*, Constable, 1933, p. 169.
19. D. N. Chester, 'Management in the Nationalised Industries', op. cit.
20. See Briggs' opening chapters in *The Birth of Broadcasting*, Vol. I of *The History of Broadcasting in the UK*, op. cit.
21. It is of course true that the Charter allows more leeway than the Act. Essentially the Charter gives the BBC freedom to pursue the objectives laid down in whatever way it thinks fit within the terms of the Charter, while the Television Act instructs the IBA to do what is set out as its duty. This is one reason why some of the crucial aspects of BBC broadcasting practice – balance, for example – are established in correspondence between the BBC and the Minister or in internal documents such as the Whitley document.
22. *Report of the Broadcasting Committee 1949* (Beveridge Committee), HMSO Cmnd. 8116, paras. 27 and 28.
23. D. N. Chester, op. cit.
24. 'After all, the system was introduced into this country more or less while the watchmen slept,' Lord Reith, 'The Facade of Public Corporations', *The Times*, March 28, 1966. Quoted by Wedell, op. cit.
25. Raymond Williams, *Television: Technology and Cultural Form*, Fontana Original, 1974, p. 22.
26. Tom Burns, 'Public Good and Communication Control' included ·in Halloran and Gurevitch (eds.), *Broadcaster/Researcher Co-operation in Mass Communication Research*, University of Leicester, 1970.

27. Raymond Williams, op. cit., p. 25.
28. *Report of the Broadcasting Committee 1925*, (Crawford Committee), HMSO Cmnd. 2599.
29. J. C. W. Reith, *Into the Wind*, Hodder and Stoughton, 1949, p. 108. See the chapter on the General Strike in Briggs, Vol. I, op. cit., for Reith's interesting statement to senior BBC staff on May 15, 1926, describing the conduct of the BBC during the Strike.
30. *Reith Diaries*, entry for May 11, 1926: 'They want to be able to say they did not commandeer us, but they know that they can trust us not to be really impartial.'
31. Letter from Baldwin to Reith, July 16, 1926. Quoted by Briggs, Vol. I, op. cit., p. 384.
32. F. Phillips before the Sykes Committee. Unpublished evidence quoted by Briggs, Vol. I, op. cit., p. 177.
33. E. G. Wedell, *Broadcasting and Public Policy*, Michael Joseph, 1968, p. 59.
34. Sir Evelyn Murray's Memorandum to the Crawford Committee on behalf of the Post Office, November 1925, para. 27. Quoted by Briggs, Vol. I, op. cit., p. 328. On the other hand, as had been made clear to the Sykes Committee by F. J. Brown speaking for the Post Office: 'We did want to be able to exercise some sort of control over the nature of programmes as a whole. If the ether was to be occupied, we hoped it would be worthily occupied. We tried to word the Licence in such a way as to give us some right of objecting.' Quoted by Briggs, Vol. I, op. cit., p. 101.
35. Restrictions on wavelengths and hours of broadcasting, for example. See Briggs, Ch. III, Vol. I, op. cit.
36. G. D. H. Cole, 'The Next Ten Years in British Social and Economic Policy'. Quoted by A. H. Hanson, *Parliament and Public Ownership*, op. cit.
37. Lord Reith: 'The Facade of Public Corporations', op. cit.
38. Lord Clarendon, first Chairman of the Governors of the BBC, in his foreword to the BBC *Handbook* of 1928. Quoted by Briggs, Vol. II, op. cit., p. 3.
39. See Oliver Whitley's memoir on Reith, *The Listener*, September 18, 1975. Reviews of the *Reith Diaries* by others give a less reverent account of the great man. See Woodrow Wyatt in the *Sunday Times*, September 21, 1975: 'Being a lunatic does not of course debar one from public office. Many lunatics like Lord Reith have remarkable ability in narrow fields and an obsessive driving force to accomplish their ends.'
40. Literally, in the case of Broadcasting House: '*Templum hoc artium et musarum* . . .'
41. *Report of the Broadcasting Committee 1925* (Crawford Committee), HMSO Cmnd. 2599.

2   Institutional Perceptions

From the earliest days of broadcasting a gulf has been apparent between the formal powers vested in Government and the realities of their disposition in practice. Looking back it can be seen that the principles and ideologies of broadcasting have emerged from day to day operations rather than the reverse, and have been decisively shaped by the professionals of an expanding industry moving into new territories of activity and influence within the licensed freedom of their original brief. Although the role of 'trustee for the national interest in broadcasting' given to the new BBC by the Crawford Committee seemed a conveniently uncontroversial one in 1926, it has been the subject of widely divergent interpretations ever since. It is these that we shall be looking at in this section and in particular those of the broadcasting organisations themselves.

The Reith Connection

The first interpretations – or perhaps more properly reinterpretations – were conditioned by the fact that the structures of national trusteeship embodied in the Governors of the BBC were imposed on an existing organisation with Reith already *in situ*. (His comment was 'the Chairman and Board are a humbug'.)[1] Having briskly engineered the departure of the first Chairman, whom he disliked, Reith set about redefining the Governors' functions for the second, more compliant, incumbent. His paper, known as the Whitley Document, contains a highly significant reinterpretation of the Crawford Committee's original brief. The original Committee recommendation suggests a public corporation 'to act as the trustee for the national interest in broadcasting', and the Charter formally installed the Governors as the constitutional embodiment of the BBC, thus as the trustees of this interest. Reith's version in the Whitley Document translates this into 'The Governors act primarily as *Trustees to safeguard the Broadcasting Service in the national interest*'. Quite a different matter one would think. This document goes on to define the duties of the Governors in ways which clearly depart, to judge from Asa Briggs' detailed account of the constitutional and legislative discussions, from the intentions of the original drafters; notably in suggesting that the Governors' responsibilities are non-executive and general, and that all major policy decisions are to be taken *with* the Director General.

> Their functions are not executive, their responsibilities are general and not particular, and they are not divided up for purposes of departmental supervision. The suggestion sometimes made that Governors should be

appointed as experts or specialists in any of the activities covered by the broadcasting service is not regarded as desirable . . . They are, subject to the responsibilities and duties laid by Parliament and the Charter upon the Postmaster General, responsible for seeing that the many purposes for which broadcasting was established . . . are carried out. With the Director General they discuss and then decide upon major matters of policy and finance, but they leave the execution of that policy and the general administration of the service in all its branches to the Director General and his competent officers. The Governors should be able to judge the general effect of the service upon the public, and subject as before mentioned, are of course finally responsible for the conduct of it.[2]

A rather similar process of institutional attrition can be seen in the matter of advisory bodies. The idea of groups external to the broadcasting organisations as sources of advice and criticism had surfaced in the discussions of the Sykes and Crawford Committees. The Sykes Committee had recommended an independent Broadcasting Board to 'inspire confidence in the public mind' and to express the conception of public service through public representation of complaints and proposals about broadcasting direct to the Post Office. This was an interesting development of the idea, current at the time, that public service was simply a convenient way of avoiding the pressures of the profit motive. It was, however, predictably and vigorously opposed by Reith who described it as 'a ghastly waste of time'.[3] The Board, under Sykes' Chairmanship, met only a few times during 1924 and was discontinued by the Post Office in 1925 on the appointment of the Crawford Committee. Reith was more cordial to the formation of the Wireless Organisations Advisory Committee in 1927, which saw its function as 'interpretation of public opinion on the subject of programmes' for the assistance of BBC management. Although shortlived, this large and loyal body effectively defused the force of Crawford's recommendation about advisory bodies which had been included in the first Charter of the BBC. This had proposed advisory bodies capable of initiating research and experiment on their own account and with direct access to the Board of Governors, an idea viewed with understandable foreboding by the broadcasters.[4] In the final result the advisory bodies that came slowly into being after 1926 were firmly the creatures of the Secretariat rather than the Board of Governors. The 'debilitating tendency to overload them with *ex officio* notables' remarked on by W. A. Robson[5] showed how swiftly BBC management killed off the idea of external criticism from advisory bodies while co-opting the form for its own ambassadorial purposes.

Although Reith played a major part in directing these lines of policy, his effective influence decreased as his view of his own role became increasingly isolated and extreme. For example, his attempts to influence decisions about the BBC's future[6] when its first Charter was due to expire in 1936 included not only detailed private discussions with the two senior civil servants at the Post Office and the Treasury, but one proposal that would have eliminated public discussion altogether, and another suggesting a small committee composed of members 'of such a sort as we would be quite happy with and sure of'.[7] When a Committee of Inquiry under Lord Ullswater[8] was appointed by the Postmaster General, he tried to interfere in the selection of its members and asked for changes in the terms of reference. He complained vigorously about the final composition of the Committee and criticised its report and recommendations. Reith's intervention was firmly repelled. Although the recommendations broadly endorsed the general lines of public service broadcasting established in 1926, they reasserted the right of the State to intervene even on questions of management, and actually recommended change in BBC internal procedures for staff representation and appointments. As the Postmaster General, no doubt smarting from BBC pressures, said in the House of Commons at the time, even an independent public corporation 'cannot in the long run defeat the House of Commons'.[9]

Monopoly Powers and the Beveridge Committee

At the same time it is possible to see in this period the emergence of the BBC as a national institution, powerfully motivated to preserve itself and its areas of influence, and able to operate effectively through personal and official contacts at the top levels of Government and the Civil Service. The failure and increasing embarrassments of Reith's megalomania were paralleled by growing organisational sophistication, a fact that may have contributed indirectly to his departure in 1938, neatly engineered by his Chairman of Governors, F. W. Norman. What was developing was broadcasting as a major social and political force, as the practice of broadcasting became a major industry and its practitioners members of an increasingly complex organisation with a widening range of interests and spheres of operation. The BBC staff increased from 773 in 1926 to 5,100 at the outbreak of war and the audience more than quadrupled in the same period. The BBC's income swelled from £183,000 in 1927 to just over £2 million in 1935 and £3½ million at the end of the decade. It was the physical scale and rate of growth of this public service as much as the legendary personality of its first Director General that set the pace of broadcasting policy.

But this expansion also threw into sharper definition the unresolved problems inherent in the relations of State and broadcasting organisation, highlighting the fragile nature of the assumptions of agreement on which the constitutional relationship were so precariously balanced. These centred during the inter-war years on sharp disagreements over finance, one of the subjects left vague in the original constitutional discussions. (Even the Ullswater Report accepted sponsored programmes as a possible source of finance without much discussion of their implications.)[10] During the war the BBC was under the direct control of the Ministry of Information and its finance was determined by the Minister – interestingly, at a level representing almost double the licence fees received. By 1949, however, with the BBC still basking in its wartime prestige, the main issue that presented itself to the Beveridge

Committee of Inquiry was the question of the monopoly power vested in this huge public corporation, and the adjustment of methods of democratic control to the unusual conditions of the broadcasting service.[11] This, though approached obliquely, can now be seen to be the first coherent public discussion of the accountability of broadcasting. Intriguingly, one of the reasons given by the Committee for the maintenance of the monopoly was that it made it easier to enforce the necessary regard to national interest and outside opinion:

> Right use of the great power of broadcasting must be safeguarded . . . We believe that it will be easier in practice to apply safeguards to one corporation than to several.
> The problem as it presents itself to us is that of devising internal as well as public and external safeguards against misuse of broadcasting power. We have to ensure that whatever authority has charge of broadcasting shall have within it effective organisation of self-criticism and of response to criticism from outside in continual operation, shall have within it a force making for increasing devolution of authority, shall have within it a force keeping access to the microphone open to all who are worthy of such responsibility. We have to ensure that, if for any reason these internal safeguards prove ineffective . . . there shall be external means . . . of bringing the failure to light and to correction.[12]

In the context of accountability, the most arresting question posed by the Committee was what was called (in the quaint terminology apparently chosen by Beveridge himself) Fundamental Question 6: '*What alternatives are there to competition and to Parliamentary control as a means of preventing broadcasting from falling into the hands of an uncontrolled bureaucracy?*'[13] Competition, as the Committee saw it, would lower standards and divert broadcasting from its 'public service for a social purpose'. Detailed parliamentary control, on the other hand, would make for timid programming, and would subject broadcasting to the influence of the particular political views dominant at one time. However, the Committee felt that further measures *were* required to prevent it 'falling into the hands of an uncontrolled bureaucracy, however good the intentions of the bureaucracy'.[14] Its recommendations, having examined the internal procedures of the BBC in very considerable detail, included not only the availability to Parliament of fuller information as to the work of the broadcasting authority, as a matter of right rather than BBC consent, but also regional production, extended functions for the Governors (involving the disappearance of the Whitley document), a Public Representation Service as an essential part of the internal management of broadcasting, and quinquennial reviews.

In one of its closing paragraphs the Report made some particularly interesting comments on the constitutional questions relevant to accountability. The largest problem, it said, was:

How a monopoly public service can be kept effectively in touch with outside opinion and at the same time can be efficiently administered within. The solution for that problem is found for Government departments in the working partnership of the political Minister and the Chief Official, usually known as the Permanent Secretary. The latter . . . maintains internal efficiency. The former, responsible for adjusting policy to public opinion, ensures that the experts do not become masters . . . On the partnership of Minister and Permanent Secretary the successful working of the Department in service to the public depends. That, in principle . . . is the solution we suggest for the broadcasting service . . . The time has come we believe to establish the Board of Governors with their Chairman as the policy framing link with the world outside the organisation. The Chairman and his Board, like the Minister, will be neither permanent nor full-time in departmental work, but . . . will collectively have unrestricted power and responsibility.[15]

Given the range of the Committee's analysis and the force of many of its criticisms, notably of the very considerable powers that had accrued to the Board of Management, the Report's recommendations are disappointingly weak. (The criticisms may have gained edge from the fact that Beveridge himself had felt unfairly prevented from discussing his social security proposals on radio in 1943.)[16] There was no doubt, though, about the impact of Selwyn Lloyd's astringent minority report. This put the case for competition in broadcasting, and demonstrated the weaknesses of the main report's own solutions to the problem of democratic control of broadcasting:

The BBC state in effect in their evidence that it is the BBC's duty to decide what it is good for people to hear or see, and that the BBC must elevate the public taste . . . National Corporations might all be staffed by good and worthy people, animated by the loftiest principles, but it would be the negation of freedom and democracy to vest in them such powers . . .[17]

The Impact of Competition and the Pilkington Report

The introduction of commercial television in 1954 had, of course, nothing at all to do with concern for the accountability of broadcasting services, little with the criticisms made by the Beveridge Committee of the BBC, and probably not very much directly with Selwyn Lloyd's case for competition. The success of the small group who masterminded the operation on behalf of advertising interests actually depended on skilful manipulation of the fears and lethargy inherent in the democratic process; and, paradoxically, on precisely the exercise of the central government powers originally retained to safeguard national interest.[18] However, one can speculate that the problems aired by Beveridge did do something to dilute the unquestioning acceptance of the BBC's identification with the national interest in broadcasting; the fact that the problems the Committee had identified remained unresolved may have

20

weakened, in some critical sense, the confidence and unanimity with which the goals of public service broadcasting were interpreted.

A critical analysis of broadcasting in the 60s noted perceptively that 'the coming of independent television increased the number of sources, but left the theory of the system unchanged.'[19] The notion of a national interest in broadcasting persisted, and so did the unexamined concept of public service. As the Pilkington Committee of 1960 remarked, 'The constitution of British broadcasting as a public service entrusted to public corporations has been shaped by the concept of the character of the service it was intended to supply.'[20] The Pilkington Committee was wrestling with the undeniable dilemmas of democratic practice in technically restricted media, but confronted as it was by the ebullient victories of commercial television, it could do no more than return to the security of the original formulations of public interest:

> the duty of the public corporations has been, and remains, to bring to public awareness the whole range of worthwhile, significant activity and experience.[21]

In spite of some cogent analysis of the structural difficulties of the ITA in resolving the conflicts of commercial interest and public service, the national interest in broadcasting was by and large taken as an identifiable and agreed goal, to be pursued by competing corporations in precisely the same spirit as it was developed by a monopoly service.

This firm and unquestioned foundation of agreed purposes, if it existed in 1960, has not survived the intervening years. Since Pilkington reported, dramatic changes have been taking place in the nature of the public discussion of broadcasting. This is most notable in the shift of attention from the details of programming and the content of programmes back to the problems of structure and governance that exercised Beveridge. Militant assaults on the broadcasting authorities launched by the broadcasting unions, academic groups and the redoubtable Viewers' and Listeners' Association have queried not only the validity of their judgments on broadcasting matters but also, most strikingly, the principles of trusteeship and consensus that have traditionally underpinned their right to make such judgments. The rest of this chapter will look at the ways in which the broadcasting authorities have responded to these changes; but before moving on it is worth examining the idea of 'independence', a key ideological concept in the debate that will be discussed more fully in the final chapter.

The Concept of Independence

'Independence' in this context is centred on the idea that broadcasting organisations should enjoy freedom from outside interference in the day to day management of their affairs. Its history is curious, and it is often forgotten

21

that in its original form it was justified almost wholly as a matter of practical convenience. Broadcasting organisations needed to enjoy, said the Crawford Committee, 'a freedom and flexibility which a Minister himself could scarcely exercise in arranging for performers and programmes and in studying the variable demands of public taste and necessity'.[22] However, by 1946 a Government White Paper reformulated the idea in the light of wartime experience of propaganda and endorsed independence on the grounds that it was 'best calculated to remove from the party in power the temptation to use the State's control of broadcasting for its own political ends'.[23] It is striking that this reasoning is an almost exact reversal of the original arguments which had recommended a licensed freedom in day to day broadcasting activities because Ministers did not want to become involved in the supervision of 'mere detail'. As the Crawford Committee saw it, broadcasting was dedicated to 'the progress of science and the harmonies of art' and could be sent on its way to do good rather in the manner of a consumer association or the RSPCA. None the less there was in the twenties a firm recognition that ultimate power and responsibility must lie with the State: indeed, this was spelt out in a fashion that today sounds positively revolutionary, so much has the balance of the argument shifted. (For example, Charles Trevelyan, a member of the Sykes Committee, wrote: 'Control over such a potential power over public opinion and the life of the nation [broadcasting] ought to remain with the State.')[24]

It is particularly interesting to see how broadcasters' views on the matter have also shifted to accommodate the changing views of Government. In Reith's day, the emphasis was on managerial efficiency, and freedom from the meddling and interference of outsiders and civil servants, an attitude that complemented the emphasis on convenience on the Government side. As the size and influence of broadcasting organisations increased, this argument for efficiency (though still maintained) has been reinforced by weightier justifications. 'Without genuine independence it is difficult, if not impossible, for broadcasters to maintain the highest standards of truthfulness and impartiality. Conversely, without having established a reputation for just those qualities it is difficult for any broadcasting organisation to be recognised as being truly independent and worthy of trust.'[25]

What this poses, however, is a neat dilemma. If the conduct of broadcasting is regarded as an unimportant matter or if the national interest in broadcasting is clearly defined and agreed by all parties, it is possible to establish the independence of broadcasters as a matter of practical convenience within the formula of Governors' and Members' trusteeship. If, however, broadcasting is held to play such a crucial role that it should be independent of Government as a *matter of principle*, then the corollary is that the processes by which public service organisations internally define the national interest become a matter of considerable concern. Awareness of this problem is reflected in the Annual Reports of the broadcasting authorities, which have in recent years begun to concern themselves with aspects of their organisations which had previously gone unnoticed.

Response from the BBC

Where the BBC is concerned, it is evident that considerable effort has gone into the rediscovery and presentation of advisory committees and even the handling of correspondence as acts of communion with the nation. It is a process that really needs to be appreciated in its progression through the annual reports of the last fifteen years, but a few excerpts only will have to suffice. In the Annual Report of 1969/70, for example, under the heading 'Public Affairs', details are given of the lunchtime lectures, which are described as 'one small corner of the BBC's system of keeping the public and itself informed about public reaction to programmes'.[26] Other facets of this system are described as 'extensive correspondence', audience research, and advisory committees. The work of the Central Religious Advisory Committee is cited as an example of the way in which advisory bodies can help influence BBC thinking, by its recommendation (accepted) that Choral Evensong should not be discontinued.

In the following year mention is made of Lord Normanbrook's important lecture on the constitutional responsibilities of the Governors, and under the same heading of Public Affairs the first mention of accountability appears:

> The role of the Governors as trustees for the public [sic] interest in broadcasting is one very important aspect of the system of control and public accountability. There are many more. The BBC's Advisory Bodies, an elaborate system of programme correspondence and investigation of complaints, public speeches by the Chairman and Members of the Board of Management, a readiness to apologise when apology is justified – all these are parts of a long-existing procedure. This Report to Parliament in itself is the most detailed demonstration, year by year, of the BBC's public accountability.[27]

The next report, again under 'Public Affairs', discusses the research report *Violence in Television* and describes the decision to set up an independent complaints commission 'to offer the BBC, with attendant publicity, a second opinion in cases of complaints where a viewer . . . continues to feel aggrieved after receiving a BBC explanation'. It also gives an account of the Governors' investigation of the *Yesterday's Men* incident, notable for its brevity. This ends:

> We shall, however, do nothing that could put at risk the independence of the BBC. Broadcast journalism has special obligations, but it cannot surrender to any individual or party or government . . . its right to impartial editorial judgment.[28]

More recently, proposals for a Broadcasting Council are discussed in the BBC *Handbook* for 1974. While this is rejected as a proposal, the Introduction comments:

This is not of course to say that the BBC remains indifferent to the considerations which have given birth to the idea of a Broadcasting Council. On the contrary, it has for some time been actively studying ways in which its already extensive machinery for keeping itself in touch with and responsive to public opinion might be improved.[29]

The general tone of these reports is carried through in BBC evidence to the Annan Committee:

> The interaction between the BBC and its public depends overwhelmingly, inescapably and rightly on the BBC's programmes. That is where the programme-maker and his [sic] audience make their most important contact, but it is not the first or the last. Our relations with the public express themselves in a number of activities complementary to the business of programme-making and presentation. These activities are themselves important because the act of programme-making arouses in members of the audience a legitimate expectation of dialogue. The audience expects a dialogue and gets it . . . It would be wrong to suppose that the BBC exists on one side of a barrier and the public on the other. In fact there is no barrier. We and the people we serve are in a relationship so close that it is difficult to draw a clear boundary between us.[30]

The Memorandum goes on to describe in detail the activities which constitute the 'continuous dialogue with the public from every level within the BBC' and which include, in a category labelled 'On Being Sensitive to the Public's Opinion', programme correspondence, audience research and advisory bodies. Lectures, complaints procedures, publicity and liaison with Parliament are also mentioned.

In the light of the history of broadcasting all this can be welcomed as a sign of incipient sensitivity to the problems of accountability and one can certainly have total sympathy with BBC concern to give a robust account of itself in difficult times. Nevertheless, the tone can hardly be said to be entirely convincing.

Counterattack from the IBA

In contrast to the cognitive dissonance of the BBC version, the IBA case has a brutally realistic edge. In its evidence to the Annan Committee it states roundly:

> In certain quarters the accountability of broadcasting organisations has been discussed virtually as an end in itself, irrespective of the service they provide; and it seems to be suggested that accountability is more important than the programme service. This seems at best an over-emphasis and at worst a device to allow judgments to be made of a broadcasting organisation without the trouble of having to watch or listen to any of its

programmes . . . the extent to which the Authority fulfils its duties is to be judged primarily by watching Independent Television and listening to Independent Local Radio.[31]

It goes on to say:

> Accountability is not always closely defined. Some people appear to see it primarily as the requirement of an organisation to provide information and to avoid secrecy; others as the liability for it to be overruled or censured after the event by some supervisory authority.

This leads to a distinction between legitimate and illegitimate demands for accountability. Legitimate demands are those that seek information: 'It is necessary', the Authority's evidence says, 'that the broadcasters should not only act reasonably but be seen to act reasonably.' Illegitimate demands, on the other hand, are those which seek greater control and want to shift the emphasis towards 'public accountability, with the implication that accountability to the public can be exercised somehow more directly than by accounting to its elected representatives'.[32]

The theoretical underpinning of this hard line on accountability can be found in an interesting article by Mary Warnock, a Member of the Authority. Writing in the second issue of *Independent Broadcasting*,[33] the IBA's house journal, she argues that accountability necessarily involves both a degree of power to impose sanctions and a general right to know. It is only where both exist that it is strictly appropriate to talk about accountability. Since the public has no sanctions to exercise against broadcasting authorities, broadcasting authorities cannot be publicly accountable. Further, the public cannot even claim a general right to know what is being done since this right 'exists only where there is a relation of power such that one can exercise some sanction over the body whose activities one is demanding to know about'.

For these reasons, Mrs Warnock concludes, only accountability to Parliament can be held to exist, and the concept of public accountability should be replaced by that of responsibility to the public. She illustrates this by reference to the NHS surgeon/patient relationship, and to the local authority/parent relationship *vis-à-vis* educational services, where she argues the relationship of responsibility, rather than accountability, exists. A concluding comment suggests that demands for accountability may stem from a kind of egalitarianism which refuses to allow anyone the role of decision-making authority:

> In this context accountability means the quite general duty to discuss every decision on equal terms with the receiving public . . . a Hobbes-like state of nature. In this sense it is better to refuse accountability and shoulder instead the more familiar burden of responsibility.

This is good crisp stuff, if somewhat insensitive in its approach to public anxieties. The IBA, however, has developed the theory a little further. Since public accountability does not exist, it argues, demands for it must actually represent an attack on the sovereignty of Parliament which, it claims incorrectly, 'has always prided itself on the fact that it does not control or even interfere in broadcasting'. The Authority continues:

> It does not seem to us that the elected representatives can be by-passed in this way, or that they would wish to substitute their own judgment . . . for that of the Members whom the Government appoints. For Members of the Authority are the means by which Independent Broadcasting is responsible to the public without being answerable to its rulers in a way which would weaken the independence which broadcasting . . . has in our society.[34]

Four Concluding Observations

By way of general comment on these institutional attitudes to the problems of accountability, four brief observations can be made before looking at institutional practice in the next chapter.

The first concerns the tone of the organisational response. There are signs of what Tom Burns has called 'latent role reversal', that is, the tendency of service occupations to carry with them a counteracting and normally concealed posture of hostility, 'wavering', as he describes it, 'between cultivated indifference and contemptuous dismissal'.[35] Although Sir Hugh Greene has noted *à propos* the responsibilities of broadcasters that if the public feels itself abused by its servants in the end the public may remove them, the force of his statement does not encourage confidence that the broadcasters will go that easily.[36]

Secondly, there is, supporting this attitude, a curiously restricted view of the function of external criticism. It might commonly be supposed that the value of external criticism of a public service lay precisely in the fact that, not sharing the assumptions and common experience of professionals inside the service, it could throw useful light on the way in which the practices and procedures were received outside. However, it appears to be considered by both the BBC and IBA as a threat; more than that, as a consistently hostile and negative force to be resisted or repelled at all costs. The techniques of resistance are more subtle than Reith's attempts to pack committees and pre-empt public discussion by private negotiations with senior Civil Servants (though they by no means exclude them) but a very similar attitude is demonstrated in the concern to contain both information and policy determination within the boundaries of the organisations concerned. The contemptuous public dismissal of a Labour Party discussion document on the future of broadcasting[37] might be considered merely an indiscretion on the part of a new BBC Chairman.[38] However, the evolution of *Broadcasting in the Seventies* and of ITV 2 policies illustrate the same process on a calculated basis, both being major proposals with national implications developed in detail without any open public opportunities for participation in the decisive stages of the debate. It can be noted that these two issues also illustrate Beveridge's bogey of the 'experts as master', since the initiatives came from the internal bureaucracies of the organisations concerned rather than the Governors or Members:

> Of necessity it was not possible to reveal all the details of each proposal at once to all interested groups, and during the period of uncertainty there were several misunderstandings,

the BBC wrote in its Annual Report fo 69/70 of *Broadcasting in the Seventies*. It continued:

> The BBC did its best to reassure all those who feared a decline in standards . . . but no reassurance seemed to be sufficient and it became clear that the BBC would have to rely on the programmes themselves . . . to convince the critics that their fears were misplaced.[39]

This in turn directs attention to the third striking characteristic common to BBC and IBA perceptions of accountability. That is, that the role of trustee for the national interest in broadcasting comes increasingly to be identified with the maintenance and defence of existing institutions. This apparently subtle alteration has the effect of pushing the trustees (that is Governors and Members) into a passive rather than an active role, chiefly concerned with repelling outside assaults on their institutions and, as Beveridge described it, 'watching the great wheels of broadcasting go round'.[40] Even accepting that the national interest in broadcasting may at a given moment reside in the IBA and the BBC, the permanent assumption of such an identification would seem a dangerous one.

Finally, there is the crucial difficulty of engaging with problems of national interest in broadcasting that overlap the institutional boundaries of the organisations concerned. This is not properly the fault of the IBA or the BBC, rather of the policy vacuum in which competitive broadcasting organisations are expected to define the national interest, but there are practical examples to illustrate the dangers of this theoretical gap. The introduction of colour television, for example, was a decision made by the BBC in fierce competition with commercial television companies. It might well have been postponed had the decision been taken with a more detached consideration of national interest at the time. Educational broadcasting, the levy and the stalemated allocation of the Fourth Channel are other examples of issues of national significance in broadcasting in which the policies of the IBA and the BBC appear to express parochial rather than general concerns.

Perhaps the most important question is that of broadcasters' independence. As we have seen, history is somewhat battered in the process of justifying, as the IBA does in its jaunty evidence to Annan, the absence of operative machinery of accountability on the grounds of sacrosanct principles of broadcasters' independence. However, even were it the case that the original legislators had wished to enshrine this principle in the constitution of early broadcasting law (which they didn't), it might still be desirable to reconsider the problems of broadcasting and its accountability and independence in the light of today's more complicated and controversial circumstances. The independence of the major social and economic forces involved in mass communication is a wider issue than merely the absence of political intervention. There may be excellent fundamental reasons for wishing to protect broadcasting – or indeed any public service – from partisan political manipulation; but equally from commercial manipulation, cultural imperialism and exploitation of sex and violence. The tendency of broadcasters to polarise the argument solely in terms of distortion of facts for political purposes does less than justice to the genuine complexity of the issues at stake. It also raises doubts about the capacity of broadcasting organisations to define the national interest on our behalf in matters in which their own interest is so clearly involved. It remains to be seen how far the machinery of 'relations with the public' affects this concern.

Notes

1. *Reith Diaries*, entry for April 16, 1927.
2. The Whitley Document is quoted in full in Lord Simon of Wythenshawe's *The BBC From Within*, Gollancz, 1953. See also the *Report of the Broadcasting Committee 1949* (The Beveridge Report) Paras. 552–555 for comments on Lord Simon's evidence to the Committee and its conclusions on the Whitley document.
3. *Reith Diaries*, entry for May 14, 1924.
4. See useful section in Asa Briggs, *The History of Broadcasting in the United Kingdom*, Vol. I, OUP, 1965, pp. 240–50.
5. W. A. Robson, 'The BBC' in W. A. Robson (ed.), *Public Enterprise*, Allen and Unwin, 1937.
6. See Briggs, op. cit., Vol. II, p. 477.
7. *Reith Diaries*, entry for March 2, 1934.
8. *Report of the Broadcasting Committee 1935* (Ullswater Report), HMSO Cmnd. 5091.
9. Debate on new BBC Charter following two previous debates on Ullswater proposals and Government White Paper during 1936, Hansard, Vol. 318.
10. Direct advertising was to be banned: 'We are most anxious that the intellectual and ethical integrity which the broadcasting system in this country has attained should be preserved.' Sponsored programmes could be allowed, on the other hand, providing they were used 'discreetly'. Ullswater Report, op. cit.
11. *Report of the Broadcasting Committee 1949* (Beveridge Report), HMSO Cmnd. 8116.
12. Beveridge *Report,* op. cit., Paras. 179/180.
13. Beveridge *Report,* op. cit., Paras. 204/205.
14. Beveridge *Report,* op. cit., Para. 306.
15. Beveridge *Report,* op. cit., Para. 617.
16. Briggs, op. cit., Vol. II, pp. 610–616.
17. Selwyn Lloyd Minority Report, in Beveridge *Report*, op. cit., p. 201, re power to destroy the *de facto* monopoly enjoyed by the BBC.
18. H. H. Wilson, *Pressure Group*, Secker and Warburg, 1961, gives an excellently detailed account of this operation.
19. Philip Abrams, chapter on 'Radio and Television' in Denys Thomson (ed.), *Discrimination and Popular Culture*, Pelican Original, 1964.
20. *Report of the Broadcasting Committee 1960* (Pilkington Report), HMSO Cmnd. 1753, Para. 23.
21. Pilkington *Report*, Para. 23.
22. Crawford *Report*, op. cit.

23. *Broadcasting Policy*, a Government White Paper on Broadcasting, 1946, HMSO Cmnd. 6852.
24. Charles Trevelyan in a minority reservation to the Broadcasting Committee: Report, 1923, HMSO Cmnd. 1951.
25. Lord Hill, Speech, April 1968, 'Freedom of the Communicator', BBC.
26. *Annual Report and Accounts* of the BBC, 1969/1970, HMSO Cmnd. 4520, p. 18.
27. *Annual Report and Accounts* of the BBC, 1970/1971, HMSO Cmnd. 4824, p. 15.
28. *Annual Report and Accounts* of the BBC, 1971/1972, HMSO Cmnd. 5111, p. 12.
29. BBC *Handbook*, 1974, p. 14.
30. BBC Memorandum for the Committee on the Future of Broadcasting, 1975. 'The BBC and the Public', p. 1.
31. IBA Evidence to the Committee of Inquiry into the Future of Broadcasting, IBA, 1974, Paras. 201 and 204.
32. Ibid., Para. 205.
33. Mary Warnock, 'Accountability, Responsibility – or Both?', *Independent Broadcasting*, No. 2, Nov. 1974.
34. IBA Evidence to the Committee of Inquiry into the Future of Broadcasting, op. cit., Para. 206.
35. Tom Burns, 'Public Service and Private Worlds' in Paul Hamos (ed.), *The Sociological Review Monograph No. 13*, University of Keele, 1969.
36. H. Carleton Greene, *The Broadcaster's Responsibility*, BBC, March 1962: 'If the public feels itself abused by its servants, in the end the public may remove them and replace them by others.'
37. *The People and the Media*, a Labour Party Discussion document, The Labour Party, 1974. See also Lord Hill's Introduction to the BBC *Handbook* 1972.
38. Sir Michael Swann, 'The Responsibility of the Governors', BBC Lunchtime Lecture, BBC Publications, October 1974.
39. *Annual Report and Accounts* of the BBC, 1969/1970, op. cit., p. 9.
40. Beveridge *Report*, op. cit., Para. 580.

3 Institutional Practice

This chapter will be considering how far the institutional perceptions of relations with the public are realised in practice; and will examine to what extent the machinery for public advice and consultation affects the determination of the national interest in broadcasting.

As the previous two chapters have attempted to demonstrate, British broadcasting is based on a legislative framework that assumes a consensus about the national interest in broadcasting embodied in the idea of 'good broadcasting'. Confidence in this consensus has, however, been steadily eroded. In the first place the size and complexity of the broadcasting industry has grown to an extent that quite simply raises more practical problems and impinges on a wider range of policy matters than the infant radio service of the 1920s had to cope with: in Stuart Hall's phrase, television has become the prism of our social discontents.[1] In the second place, this growth has provoked doubts about the capacity of a simple formula to encompass the many aspects of national interest that may be involved in broadcasting: the rights of individuals, questions of national resource allocation,[2] the value of investment in educational broadcasting, the influence of multi-national mass media conglomerates and choice of technologies for the future, to name but a few examples. Finally, the concept of broadcasters' independence, briefly referred to in the previous chapter, has been developed from a matter of practical convenience into a principled challenge to the original idea of ultimate accountability to the State. In part this can be seen as an expression of the self-confidence of a powerful new professional elite; but it is also the reflection of genuine uncertainties about the way mass communications should be handled in democratic societies.

The particular significance of the question of independence is its connection with accountability. Once independence from parliamentary supervision and involvement is claimed it becomes necessary for public service broadcasters to demonstrate how they arrive at their interpretations of the national interest; as we have seen this has led to a new emphasis on the formerly neglected bits and pieces of administrative machinery accumulated over the years – advisory bodies, publications and the like[3] – as well as the key roles of Governors and Members as trustees of the national interest. Of the two slightly different versions presented by the broadcasting organisations, the BBC broadly endorses the Pilkington view that the constitution of broadcasting reflects the concept of public service it was intended to supply, concluding that the organic harmony of national interest and institutional purpose is reflected in its existing organisation – 'a relationship with the public we serve so close . . .

that it is impossible to draw a clear boundary between us'.[4] The IBA's more rigorous view accepts only the legal obligation 'to see that broadcasters act reasonably and are seen to act reasonably', adding as an important though cautious rider that 'decision making should not be handicapped by lack of information about the public's feelings and wishes'. (In both of these there are interesting suggestions of a special relationship denied to Parliament, as if to establish a rival public interest as distinct from the national interest. Charles Curran has actually made a highly significant reference to 'authority without politics'.)[5]

To start with it is useful to look at the position of BBC Governors and Members of the Authority to which all questions of accountability are ultimately related.

Governors and Members

The Governors of the BBC *are* the BBC to the extent that its corporate identity is legally vested by Royal Charter in the Board. The original number of BBC Governors was five – in itself a demonstration of the role they were expected to play, or perhaps more accurately, an indication of the relatively unimportant and non-controversial matters for which they were to be responsible. It has already been noted that the first BBC Board inherited a going concern with an active Director General, and had to labour under the psychological and practical limitations that this imposed on their freedom of action.[6] The number of BBC Governors has now been increased to twelve, including the Chairman. The Governors are formally appointed by the Queen in Council; in practice this has meant the Postmaster General (since 1974 the Home Secretary) after consultation with political colleagues and usually the BBC itself.[7] Though the BBC Secretariat stresses that no formal consultation takes place, there are usually discussions of an informal kind between the Director General, a Senior Official, the Chairman of the Board and the responsible Minister at which 'names come up'.[8] An informal system of veto can therefore be held to exist where Governors (and sometimes Chairmen) are concerned.

The Post Office (and the Home Office now probably follows the practice) has traditionally routed the discussion of Governors' appointments through to the Chief Whip's Office. In the view of a former senior BBC official, it is the Chief Whip who plays the central role in co-ordinating political interests, BBC views and Treasury list suggestions.[9] The latter, described by the same person as 'a caprice reflecting the spirit of the time' is the collection of the names of the Great and the Good which supplies the nominees for government appointments of this kind to make sure that 'the right chaps are in the right places'.[10] Where the BBC is concerned this has included seeing that one place on the Board is normally occupied by a Foreign Office nominee (who in at least one case was directly proposed to the Whip's Office).[11] There has also been what the BBC describes as an 'unwritten convention which provides for trades union, financial and educational interests to be represented as well'.[12]

The point about this is that it emphasises not so much undesirable political interference, but rather the close nature of the relationship with establishment politics that the BBC has always maintained.

The Members of the Independent Broadcasting Authority are the Authority in the same legal sense that the Governors are the BBC. Just as the Charter specifies in some detail the appointment and duties of Governors, giving only passing mention to the appointment of 'such officers and staff as it may from time to time consider necessary',[13] so the Television Act concentrates on the Authority's composition and duties, leaving it to determine for itself the detail of the service 'alternative to that of the BBC and of high quality' that it is required to provide for the public. While spelling out the disqualifications in more detail, the constitutional position of Members of the Authority set out in the Act is essentially that of BBC Governors. There is now a maximum of 13 members, including the Chairman and Deputy Chairman, and the procedure for their appointment is similar to that described above. Both the Board of Governors and the Authority include three members with individual concern for Scotland, Wales and N. Ireland and special responsibility for programming in their areas. According to George Wedell, on its creation in 1954 the Authority 'proceeded on the assumption that its relationship would be analogous to that established between their respective opposite numbers at the BBC'.[14]

The appointments of both Members and Governors have always been part-time, precluding a detailed executive role. Although the Chairmanship is considered to require the major part of the incumbent's time and attention, it is not regarded or paid as a full-time post.[15] It is difficult to establish as a matter of fact, but examination of the membership of the BBC's Board of Governors and the Authority suggests that the Board may still rank slightly higher than the Authority in terms of the importance attached to its membership by Governments of both parties.[16]

The functions of the Board and Authority were described by Pilkington as follows:

> We reiterate that the Governors' and Members' concern is to represent and secure the public interest in broadcasting. It is for them to judge what the public interest is, and it is for this that they are answerable . . . Their task is, as we have said, to be thoroughly aware of public opinion in all its variety, to care about it and to take proper and full account of it. Having done so, they must identify the public interest in broadcasting, defined as the fullest possible realisation of the purposes of broadcasting, and secure it through control of the executive arm.[17]

The Report went on to say of Governors and Members that:

> They must ensure that, so far as possible, policies are translated into programming fact. They must know and care about public opinion; but in appraising and interpreting it, they must represent the public conscience.[18]

Though admirably expressing the intention of successive Governments since the war, this less successfully engages with the practical problems of the Governors' and Members' tasks. Historically it is in action that policy has always been created, as a former senior staff member of the BBC observed.[19] The first Board of the BBC was subservient to its Director General, Reith, and so was the first Authority to Sir Robert Fraser. The line of acquiescent BBC Chairmen was broken by Sir Ernest Simon in 1947 (later Lord Simon of Wythenshaw), who was unable to accept the Whitley document's interpretation of his duties and helped to persuade the Beveridge Committee that the Board should 'perform effectively the functions of a Minister in keeping his department in touch with public opinion and subject to external criticism. The channel for informed democratic control of broadcasting must lie with the Governors'.[20] The view of a Postmaster General ten years later was that the Governors were still unable to exercise any real influence, and appeared to be governed by the professionals.[21] Lord Normanbrooke, Chairman of the BBC from 1964 until 1967, wrestled with these problems and concluded reluctantly that the practical complexity of broadcasting administration forced the Board in most cases to exercise their control 'by retrospective review – by comment, whether praise or blame, after the event'.[22] These practical difficulties are even more intense for the members of the Authority, who are forced to rely on the expertise of IBA staff to keep them in touch with the programming problems of 15 ITV companies. It is interesting none the less to note that they have on occasion been prepared to impose positive vetoes on programming; e.g., ATV's *South of the Border*, and *World In Action's* Poulson coverage, and to give public (if not altogether satisfactory) reasons for these actions.

The practical problems of handling, on a part-time and lay basis, the intricate policies of broadcasting management are compounded by the nature of the selection process and the bodies that are produced by them, which have been predominantly middle-class, middle-aged and until recently male.[23] The size of the Board and Authority makes any 'representative' requirement difficult, though categories of essential membership are now recognised. The original desire for 'persons of judgment and independence' expressed by the Crawford Committee is impeccable; however, the procedures over the years have produced groups of people of total respectability and similar social background, with the addition, in recent years, of statutory trades union representatives. The comparatively low fees offered and the burden of work imposed on Governors and Members is in itself a severe restriction on the range of people able to take on the work. 'The Establishment is democracy's working party', Sir Robert Fraser has neatly observed.[24] This problem is not of course confined to broadcasting since many areas of British administration have depended in the past on the amateur principle for 'democratic' initiative. However, it is not clear that salaries or higher fees will provide a solution. Similarly, the part-time principle was specifically embodied in the specification for Governors and Members to avoid 'becoming part of the Executive and so ceasing effectively to represent the public interest'.[25] But as has been very perceptively noted by George Wedell, part-time governors are usually less well informed than full-time officials, and likely to let awareness of their amateur status give the benefit of the doubt to the professionals. In this way a 'cumulative commitment develops which can be disowned later only with difficulty'.[26]

Finally, there is the problem that Governors and Members necessarily depend for information, organisation, communication and in some sense for their corporate identity on the secretariats of the organisation they supervise.[27] Governors and Members are not usually well known as such to the general public, and apart from the two Chairmen they normally refrain from public statements about broadcasting. Even private discussions about broadcasting issues are considered by some Governors and Members to break the rules of confidentiality and corporate responsibility.[28] These difficulties seem particularly acute at the BBC, probably because of the direct connection between the Board and the executive operations of the BBC. It is not widely known, for example, that as a matter of principle Governors' personal addresses are not disclosed by the BBC. All correspondence must normally be addressed to them at Broadcasting House, where unless marked 'personal' it is opened by the BBC secretariat and may or may not be forwarded on with comments attached to the letters; this was the case at least until 1973.[29]

Yesterday's Men and the Warhol Affair

In this connection the handling of *Yesterday's Men* and the Warhol Affair is of particular interest as an illustration of the constraints within which Governors and Members have to operate. *Yesterday's Men* was the notorious BBC programme of June 17, 1971 which, breaking with tradition, gave several senior Labour Party politicians – including Harold Wilson – satirical treatment accompanied by pop songs and cartoons in a programme slot normally reserved for straight political coverage. Not only did the participants feel that they had been unfairly ridiculed, but they also accused the BBC of 'carefully calculated, deliberate and continuous conceit over a period of months' in concealing the title and style of the programme from those who took part in it. The BBC, on its side, while admitting minor mistakes in the handling of the programme, publicly took its stand on the principle of the independence of the BBC and its right to 'impartial editorial judgment'. In the event, the programme produced great glee amongst young broadcasters, mixed reactions in the Press, outrage at Labour Party headquarters and a first class row at the BBC, the consequences of which have been far reaching.

Two aspects of the affair are worth recording here. (For a more detailed account of the events reference should be made to the detailed study by Michael Tracey of the Centre for Mass Communication Research at the University of Leicester.[30]) First is the fact that the Governors were involved at the last minute in the controversial editorial decision to transmit the programme. Harold Wilson had complained about questions asked in an interview for the programme and demanded deletions. A compromise was reached after negotiation, but Director General Charles Curran felt that it required the ratification of the Governors 'if only', according.to Tracey, 'because of the fuss that was likely to ensue'.[31] On the day of proposed transmission Curran therefore showed the film to the Chairman of Governors (Lord Hill) and a few of the Governors who happened to be around. Later in the day Lord Hill asked the Governors as a body whether they thought the film should go ahead as planned, and transmission was endorsed by the Governors though not all of them had seen it. *Yesterday's Men* was thus shown on the evening of June 17 with Governors' approval.[32]

As a result of the controversy the BBC felt obliged to institute an internal inquiry conducted by two senior members of BBC staff. A second but less widely known aspect of the affair is that the Labour Party submitted a formal complaint addressed to the Governors, and delivered by hand to Broadcasting House, which was never received by them. The complaint was in the form of a 3,000 word document prepared by Wilson's legal advisors on behalf of the Labour Party. Joe Haines, Wilson's Press Secretary, later complained in *The Guardian* that this report was delayed by the BBC and did not reach the Governors until their meeting over a fortnight later. The verdict of the BBC's inquiry, he concluded, accompanied rather than followed the evidence.[33] The truth of the matter seems to be that the Governors never received the original Labour Party document *at all*. What it appears they did receive was the internal BBC report (incorporating the Labour Party complaints along with other evidence received) together with a draft Governors' statement on the affair prepared by Lord Hill. Thus the evidence did not accompany the verdict, it was already subsumed in the internal inquiry's report and conclusions.

These incidents throw into sharper focus the problems of trusteeship facing Governors. They were not only totally dependent for servicing and information on the organisation they were supposed to be supervising, but were also drawn smoothly into complicity in events and actions that they had little opportunity to control or direct. When the matter of *Yesterday's Men* came to a crisis the Governors were ill informed, swiftly compromised, and firmly organised to fight a rearguard action in defence of the BBC. They had allowed themselves to be involved at the last moment in a controversial editorial decision in total conflict with the reigning Normanbrooke principle of retrospective review. They were then required to sit in judgment on that editorial decision. Finally, they apparently received evidence only after it had been processed by staff of the organisation they were supposed to be examining on the public's behalf. It is difficult to reconcile these facts with the Governors' evidence to the Annan Committee which proclaims their function to be that of 'critic and guardian of the broadcasters'.[34] As Lord Hill has since admitted in his Memoirs, 'The more we were seen in this defensive role, the more difficult it was to be seen to be, if not actually to be, the trustees for the public.'

A slightly different light – though equally illuminating – is thrown on the trustees' role by the Warhol Affair, in which Members of the Authority found

35

themselves embarrassingly embroiled in 1973. Again, the progress of events is complicated, involving not only the whole question of television 'censorship' and the role of the Authority in enforcing the Television Act, but also an important legal principle concerning the right of individual citizens to challenge the action of public authorities without necessarily obtaining the support of the Attorney General. The plot was further thickened by the appearance of Mrs Whitehouse, moral crusader; David Bailey, society photographer and maker of the film at issue; Andy Warhol, subject of the film and the source of gnomic statements in New York; a fat lady who appeared in the film taking off her clothes and painting pictures with her breasts; and Jimmy Vaughan, an art film dealer with the British distribution rights to Warhol films who shrewdly tipped off the press that a 'pornographic shocker' was about to be shown on British screens throughout the land.

The film in question, *Warhol, artist and film maker*, was commissioned from David Bailey by ATV's Factual Programme Department and production started early in 1972. During the summer of 1972 the film was edited and discussed informally at regular meetings with staff of the IBA, as a result of which various alterations and cuts were made. It was scheduled for transmission as a Tuesday Documentary, a mandatory programme which all ITV companies were required to show. However, shortly before its scheduled transmission date press stories appeared warning the public that viewers were about to see 'what many will consider to be the most permissive shocker to be shown on British screens' (*Sunday Mirror*, January 14, 1973). On the basis of these stories, though without having seen the programme himself, Ross McWhirter, an active member of the National Viewers' and Listeners' Association, sought an injunction to restrain the IBA from transmitting the film. This was refused by a High Court Judge (on the grounds that such action to defend the public interest could only be taken by the Attorney General) but was later temporarily granted by the Court of Appeal on a 2 to 1 majority. The point made by McWhirter was that there was evidence from the press reports that the film would contravene the Television Act by being offensive to public feeling, and that the Authority had not even bothered to look at it. Lord Denning agreed, saying that the evidence 'led inevitably to the inference that the programme would offend good sense and decency and offend public feelings'. (*Times* Law Report, January 16, 1973) There was therefore, the Appeals Court felt, ground for granting time to examine the issues involved.

In the final event the Court discharged the interim injunction on a technicality, endorsing the IBA's role as censor of ITV programmes. 'The Authority were the people who mattered. They were the censors. The courts had no right whatever . . . to interfere with their decisions so long as they were in accordance with the law.' (*Times* Law Report, February 5, 1973) All three judges did, however, express amazement that the IBA had in fact concluded that the film contained 'Nothing likely . . . to be offensive to public feeling', and McWhirter was right in concluding that he lost by a whisker. A crucial point in the judgment was that Members of the Authority had finally agreed to see the film themselves (something that they had resisted in defence of the professional judgment of the IBA staff) and that the film had also been shown to the General Advisory Committee. (When the original temporary injunction was granted, said Lord Denning, 'It appeared . . . that there was a *prima facie* case for saying that they had not done what was reasonably sufficient to satisfy themselves that so far as possible there was nothing indecent or offensive in the programme.') This had now been put right, the Court felt, by the hasty screenings arranged in the interim, and the virtually unanimous approval of the film that they produced. (Only one member of the General Advisory Council went on record as opposing the screening of the film on the grounds of its indecency.) The Court was also impressed by the evidence produced to show that the Members of the Authority and the 18 members of the General Advisory Council were responsible persons whose judgment of 'public feeling' could be accepted as reasonable. Lord Denning commented:

> The General Advisory Council were drawn from a broad cross section of the people and were as representative and responsible a body as one would find anywhere. The Council by a majority of 17 to one passed a resolution that the staff were right to advise the Authority that the film which they had seen was suitable to be shown at the suggested time. The Members of the Authority were likewise most representative and responsible. Ten of the 11 Members saw the film and unanimously reaffirmed the decision that the programme is suitable for transmission in the 10.30 documentary slot and that it is satisfied that the programme complies with the requirements of section 3(1)(a). If those decisions were to be accepted as valid, they were decisive. His views did not matter unless they did show that the Authority had misdirected themselves, or had come to a conclusion to which they could not reasonably come. (*Times* Law Report February 5, 1973)

Chairmen and Director Generals

These cautionary tales draw attention to the key role of the Chairman, and in particular to the relationship between him or her and the Director General. It has been suggested that 'the widely held view that this relationship is the key determinant of broadcasting policy underlines the private and inaccessible nature of important decision making in broadcasting'.[35]

It is certainly true that the nature of the post, which demands that, in Pilkington's words, broadcasting should be the 'first but not only concern',[36] sets the Chairman apart from the other Governors. A former member of senior BBC staff who had the opportunity to observe the relationship at close quarters has remarked that though the precise relationship varied from Chairman to Chairman and Director General to Director General, their significant privilege was private access to each other. This in turn determined the character of the meetings of the Board of Governors and the Board of Management: 'the essence was in these private meetings.'[37] By the same token, private meetings of Governors without the Director General's presence, as occurred under Lord Hill's Chairmanship at the BBC, have always been construed as a defeat for the Director General.

The fluctuating battlelines that have been drawn in the power struggles of this relationship can be seen in the various analogies that have been used to describe it. 'From the beginning,' says George Wedell, 'Reith could not help acting . . . like a headmaster in relation to his school governors.'[38] His first Chairman Lord Clarendon had suggested that his role as Chairman should be regarded as that of Commander-in-Chief of an army, which Reith had countered by the rather more convincing analogy of Cabinet at home with himself as Commander-in-Chief in the field.[39] The Beveridge Committee preferred the less aggressive parallels of Minister and Permanent Secretary[40] which the Pilkington Committee broadly accepted.[41] Sir Hugh Greene (more enthusiastically a Director General than a Governor) has on the other hand described the Governors as having the powers of a constitutional monarch 'to advise, to encourage and to warn', as Harold Nicholson said of George V, with additional powers over senior appointments and sackings, leaving the Director General in the Prime Minister's position.[42] (This is a definition which seems to fit the early period of the ITA pretty well.) The present Chairman of the BBC, Sir Michael Swann, has provided the most recent and disarming description. Some people had accused him of back seat driving, he said, but he saw his job as sitting up front beside the driver and reading the map.[43]

The central dilemma of the Chairman's role is clear enough. Making sound policy judgments involves a degree of knowledge and information that can only be gained by close contact with broadcasters and their work. This may lead to an involvement with executive problems and decision making that conflicts with the need for a detached external view. In this connection the IBA structure would appear to offer advantages in that it is separated physically and organisationally from the production sectors of the industry it supervises, whereas the BBC Board is not. However, the psychological context in which the first Authority operated was such that its concerns and responsibilities were overwhelmed by the danger of the early struggles for survival and the euphoria of the triumphs that followed. This was well expressed by an ITA executive of the time who described how the early days of ITV saw the emergence of:

> a small group of men bound to each other, not by any institutional feeling at all, but simply by the fact that as a group they had faced the blizzard, virtually seen the whole thing collapse and had then come through with great success. A guess would be that from then on until the 1964 Act ITV was largely run on the telephone by Lew Grade, Howard Thomas, Paul Adorian and Bob Fraser.[44]

It is also true that the Authority is dependent in a direct way on the financial viability of the companies that provide its income, a not insignificant fact.

The other side of this problem is that outside criticism, if too detached from the feelings and professional experience of the industry it is concerned with, simply becomes irrelevant interference. (This criticism has been made of the

Authority.) The dilemma has been well stated by Pilkington, though interestingly enough in a paragraph dealing with the proposal for a broadcasting council.

> But . . . the Council could not expect to acquire . . . intimate knowledge of the organisations or to enjoy . . . the confidence of the executive. If it did not, its annual report would lack the constructive element in criticism. If however it did, then it would not remain so far dissociated from the broadcasting organisations as to serve its intended purpose.[45]

As a matter of historical fact the problems of the governance of broadcasting have never presented themselves in quite this even-handed way. Overwhelmingly the governing bodies have accepted the dynamic of the institutions they are most closely associated with, whose work they study and for whose output they must accept responsibility. That 'policy is made in practice' deserves repetition. ITV 2 and *Broadcasting in the Seventies*, the IBA's campaign for the reduction of the Levy, the transfer of ITV education programmes to morning from afternoon against the wishes of schools, the extraordinary conduct of the BBC Governors over *Yesterday's Men*, are all examples of the tendency of broadcasting authorities to identify their interests, and by implication the national interest, very closely with the survival of the organisations they supervise. It is perhaps even more significant that the rare cases of public dissociation from BBC action by a Chairman[46] have provoked a storm of internal outrage.

The identification is so close and so consistent that it does indeed raise concern about the intended purpose of safeguarding the national interest. It is noteworthy, for instance, that the evidence of the BBC Board of Governors to the Annan Committee (quoted above) is presented as one part of the voluminous evidence from the BBC itself. While this may be consistent with constitutional practice in the past[47] and indeed with the constitutional position of BBC Governors as the embodiment of the Corporation as a whole,[48] it reinforces the view that were the national interest in broadcasting to require changes in existing organisations – a thinkable proposition – it would be difficult for the Governors to express them. It may be that the three tier structure of commercial broadcasting which makes a clear separation between the Authority, its executive secretariat (the IBA) and the administration of the broadcasting companies, offers major advantages in this respect, the historical camaraderie of the masters and servants notwithstanding.[49]

Advisory Committees

It is in confrontation with this problem that the machinery of relations with the public – the BBC's 'continuous dialogue' and the IBA's more carefully defined processes of public relations and research – must be considered. George Wedell's opinion is that the constitutional emphasis has always been placed on 'extensive and broadly based public control',[50] deriving this view from the emphasis in the Charter and Act on the advisory bodies that were originally seen by the Crawford Committee as an essential part of the public corporation operation of broadcasting. However, there is considerable ambiguity in the use of the term, and the idea of the advisory committee should not be confused with the idea of 'citizen consumer' representation that had been raised by the Webbs.[41] This was a matter of representation at policy making level, and sharply differentiated from the lower level advisory function. It was essentially concerned with counterbalancing the particular interest of worker representation in monopoly state concerns with 'general' public representation, a point of some subtlety.

In the event, as has been described in the previous chapter, the advisory bodies actually created have a different practical emphasis. Firstly, they are closely involved with the Secretariat and the Executive rather than the Governors. Secondly, they were initially specialist bodies organised to proffer advice on those matters on which full-time staff might not have the expert knowledge required. To this is now added the idea of a sounding board of mainstream opinion on controversial matters, but there is no question of research or development of ideas. Thirdly, and this was emphasised by the creation of the General Advisory Council in 1934, the BBC from the beginning conceived their function as ambassadorial as well as advisory, 'helping towards a fuller understanding of the BBC's problems and policy'.[52] Their membership reflected this, and even the Ullswater Committee felt forced to comment that it was desirable to secure representation for the views of the general public, not only for those 'of recognised leaders in their respective spheres or professions,' and 'celebrated teachers and exponents of the arts'.[53] Ullswater in fact introduced a new concept of 'listener interest' to the consideration of advisory bodies – 'an interest which we regard as vital is the benefit of listeners . . . We are anxious to secure the representation of the views of the general public as well as experts . . . We recommend that the membership of the Advisory Committees should be as comprehensive and varied as possible'.[54]

This idea is taken up again by the Beveridge Committee: 'Self criticism should be a function of the broadcasting authority as vital as is the production of broadcasts.'[55] Beveridge's solution is a Public Representation Service with a Director of the Corporation at its head which would be wholly concerned with stimulating external criticism and advice, servicing advisory committees and feeding the views in to the executive departments.[56] The Director would also report direct to the Governors, though Lord Simon, himself a most critical Chairman, thought this would be both difficult and invidious.[57] What is interesting about this suggestion is that the Committee did not return to the simpler original idea of the Crawford Committee (or indeed the first Charter) in which the consultation of public opinion was seen as part of the Governors' rather than the Executive's function. It would place trustees of the national interest in an awkward position if the bodies they supervise had their own access to public opinion through separate channels – a problem not unknown to the IBA, who have considerable experience of ratings used in this way.[58]

In its evidence to the Annan Committee in 1975 the BBC stresses that its advisory arrangements directly relate to the obligation resting upon the Board of Governors 'to keep themselves aware of, and to interpret, public opinion, to see from the outside the performance of the organisation for which they are responsible; and to expound and explain their policies . . . In short,' the Memorandum says, 'the advice which is proffered by these Advisory Councils and Committees assists the Governors in the discharge of their stewardship.'[59]

The BBC in 1975 had 52 committees involving 850 men and women 'from many walks of life'.[60] The functions of the Committees can be broken down into two broad groups: those which are invited to advise on policy and programmes in general, and those with a more specialised function and membership. The first group includes the General Advisory Council, the N. Ireland Advisory Council and the eight English Regional Advisory Councils. The specialist bodies include committees giving advice on a wide range of subjects ranging from charitable appeals (jointly with the IBA), music, agricultural programmes and broadcasting to Asian immigrants. As might be expected, the main problem of arranging for effective public criticism of national services arises where general rather than particular policies are concerned. As John Scupham has remarked from the vantage point of a retired senior staff member, the problem of liaison with the community is comparatively simple where programmes are designed with specific purposes for well-defined audiences with authoritative interpreters of those purposes.[61] It is far less tractable where contact has to be established with the general public over the general programme output. Even within these terms, however, the enclaves of specific and non-controversial service cannot be marked out with confidence; education and frequency allocation, for instance, though traditionally seen as residing safely in an a-political sphere of specialist professional opinion, have now moved smartly into the centre of public debate. Thus the agenda-setting role of the Secretariat is itself likely to be the subject of criticism and it is not clear within the terms of the present system how this can be subjected to effective external or internal examination.

The IBA's system of advisory bodies is similarly an expression of an informal requirement, 'to ascertain the national interest by taking account of public opinion'.[62] Section 9 of the Television Act of 1964 formally provides for the appointment at the discretion of the Authority of a General Advisory Council and other advisory bodies to 'give advice to the Authority and programme contractors on such matters as the Authority may determine'. More specifically, three specialist committees are required to handle religious matters, advertising and education. Section 24 of the Act imposes a further general obligation:

The functions of the Authority shall include the making of arrangements for bringing the programmes (including advertisements) . . . and the other activities of the Authority under constant and effective review, and in particular for ascertaining the state of public opinion concerning the programmes (including advertisements) broadcast by the Authority and for encouraging the making of useful comments and suggestions by members of the public; and the arrangements shall include provision for full consideration by the Authority of the facts, comments and suggestions so obtained.[63]

In fact the Authority before 1964 had only the three specialist committees required of it under the Act, and only set up its General Advisory Council in 1964. In March 1974 the Authority had some 16 advisory bodies involving some 250 men and women. Additional local advisory bodies are being created for new independent local radio stations as they are established. As in the BBC, the advisory bodies cover both general matters in the General Advisory Council and National Committees, and specialist topics in committees such as the Medical Advisory Panel and Schools Committee.

In considering the work of these committees in some detail, two central problems have to be examined. Can the committee's membership be regarded in any sense as representative of the national interest? If not, what is it able to contribute to Governors' and Members' interpretation of the national interest? Where membership is concerned, the Authority has gone to some pains to differentiate its policy ('We have always tried to avoid making our GAC an establishment body') from that of the BBC ('50 names picked out of *Who's Who*').[64] 'Advisory Committees cannot by themselves, however appointed, provide a fully representative cross-section of public opinion', says the Authority. 'The size to which a committee must be limited makes this impossible.' The IBA General Advisory Council 'differs from the BBC's body in that, while some members are chosen for their eminence in aspects of public life, the majority come from a wider cross-section of the viewing public and are chosen not as representatives of particular organisations but as individuals who have or will develop a critical interest in broadcasting'.[65] Discussion with members of the Committee confirms the impression of an able and independent group representing a wide spread of middle-class opinion. As is rare among committees, it has obtained an equal representation for women. The problem of obtaining representation for working-class women remains unresolved, in spite of the token female cigar factory examiner from Glasgow who figured amongst recent membership.

The contrast with BBC selection procedures is confirmed by comparison of the two General Advisory Bodies. The superbia of the BBC's General Advisory Council is striking. Even the 'fork-lift driver' paid casual reference in a lunchtime lecture turns out to be:

The Rev. Tony Williamson, MA; fork-lift driver; Chairman and Deputy Chief shop steward of the TGWU at BLMC Car Body Plant, Cowley, Oxford; Member, Oxford City and County Councils; Chairman, Oxford City Housing Committee; priest, Church of England; Member, BBC Radio Oxford Local Radio Council . . .

The significant fact about membership is of course that it is determined by the parent authorities and, effectively, by their Secretariats. The Business Committee of the BBC's General Advisory Council (itself a small executive group selected by the Secretariat) suggests categories of suitable membership and now has the right to nominate a small proportion of the total on its own account for final selection and approval by Governors. The rest are nominated by the BBC Secretariat, which also selects the Chairman. Similarly, the Authority receives nominations for advisory body membership from its Secretariat, though its General Advisory Council elects its own Chairman. However intelligently and adventurously chosen such a membership will always tend to reflect (if not consciously echo) the broadcasting organisations' general view of their own interest. As the Chairman of the BBC's General Advisory Council has wittily remarked, 'It is seldom wise to take advice from someone who wishes you had not been born.'[66]

If an energetic critic penetrates the system, the chances are that the two year term (renewable at the secretariat's discretion) will allow him or her to be shuffled off the stage before damage is done or disturbance created. It has also been pointed out by a former member of the BBC GAC that within a group of sixty it takes time to make a coherent criticism felt: the amorphous whole has a capacity to muffle particular parts and cancel out astringent views in the rhubarb of sixty voices engaged in unstructured discussion. 'An element of charade'; 'We were giving advice which would not be taken if it were unwelcome'; 'One opinion was always counterbalanced by another'; 'the critical views were dropped in the wastepaper basket'; one of the IBA's specialist panels was 'using important people almost as stooges'; 'an establishment sort of body'; GAC members are not consumers of television'; 'We were deliberately chosen not to represent a coherent point of view'.[67] These are some of the critical voices of members and former members of the two GACs, though it is only fair to say that they represented a minority of the people interviewed, who in general enjoyed the job and felt themselves useful.

Unease grows as the theme is developed. 'We appreciate that the Council can be truly effective only if it has the trust and confidence of the BBC', says the BBC's General Advisory Council in its evidence to the Annan Committee.[68] Insulated in the confidentiality rule, this sort of relationship too easily becomes cosy. 'Flattery vitiates the advice given: they had ways of making me feel important' was the comment of one former member and this aspect of the advisory bodies was taken up by the Select Committee on Nationalised Industries in a report on the IBA. In this report the IBA's General Advisory Council was specifically criticised as lacking in independence, without funds of its own, and, on its own admission, anonymous and inaccessible to the public.[69] In retrospect it seems rather a harsh judgment of a body that is certainly rather better manned and more alert than the system could reasonably expect to obtain on its present basis.

An even more worrying feature of the GAC membership gets little attention. That is, in the words of one former member of the IBA General Advisory Council, that 'they want "ordinary people" and resent special knowledge as a

43

threat to the easy supremacy of resident officials'.[70] Amongst the highly intelligent, open-minded and helpful people interviewed for this study, there was a disturbing lack of knowledge about the nature of the current debates on broadcasting. The members of the IBA GAC in 1973, for instance, were not apparently aware of the range of different views and options that had been publicly presented on the question of allocation of the Fourth Channel, and had been happy to discuss and approve the issue solely in terms of the ITV 2 proposals presented to them by the IBA. Neither did they know what networking was, though it was encouraging to discover that they asked for this to be explained. Even more remarkably, an experienced member of the BBC's GAC was not aware of the public service obligations of commercial television.

Assuming then that the selection systems operated by the authorities and their Secretariats assemble the mix of membership they consider most useful, without pretending to 'representation' of the national interest in any sense, how can these bodies be said to assist the processes of its interpretation? The organisational difficulty remains that the bodies themselves depend for their corporate identity on the Secretariats. Although Lord Hill at the IBA proposed a measure of independence for the first General Advisory Council – which would have made a most interesting experiment – in the event, as in the BBC, the committees and councils are housed, entertained, brought together and organised by the Secretariat of the parent organisation. A. H. Hanson has remarked on the psychological significance of these matters in connection with the consumer councils of nationalised industries: to the extent that they literally provide the context of the advisory bodies' discussions they are significant determinants of the nature of the discussions that take place.

Another problem is the frequency of meetings: in the case of the GACs, four times a year; in the case of specialised committees usually two or three annually. There is a genuine conflict between the need to ensure wide regional representation and full attendance and the desire for longer and more frequent meetings. One IBA GAC member remarked that 'more frequent meetings would make us less representative'. However, it is evident that the need to fit business into these four annual sessions tends to formalise the agenda to a high degree for the GACs. Both GACs hold afternoon meetings, after a lunch provided for them. The BBC GAC starts with questions and written BBC answers and supplementaries; then Matters Arising and a summary of public reaction to the previous three months' programmes, followed by the Director General's report. The main subject of the day is usually introduced by a written report from the Secretariat circulated in advance. Topics have included the Role of the GAC, Violence, Taste and Standards, internal guidelines on current affairs and documentaries, and Britain at Work. Papers from specialist committees may be circulated at the discretion of the Chairman. The Business Committee meets twice in between the main meetings to guide the Chairman and Secretariat in the preparation of the agenda and check the documentation in draft form. The Director General and senior staff are always in attendance plus 'a sprinkling of Governors who tend to fade away after lunch'.[71]

The IBA meetings start with morning screenings of programmes. After lunch and discussion of matters raised by the Steering Committee, the main business of the day is a discussion of a topic selected as being part of 'a systematic examination of public concern'. The discussions are based on papers by the IBA Secretariat (or occasionally an individual member) circulated in advance. Subjects have included Violence, Drama, News, Children's Programmes, Balance and Extended Hours. At one time the ratings were presented, but now no regular report is tabled. The meeting is attended by the Director General and Senior Staff, but not by Members of the Authority at the GAC's specific request. Since the Select Committee on Nationalised Industries' criticism of the procedures, the GAC Chairman reports directly to the Governors at their next meeting.

A perceptive comment from a member of long standing of the BBC's GAC suggests that these brief and structured meetings make it impossible for the GAC to take full advantage of the Secretariat. In other words there is not time to gain access to and discuss all the relevant information that should and could be made available. Unanimous praise has been given to the BBC documentation provided for the GAC: indeed there was general agreement, with only a few dissenting voices, at Governor and Member level as well as amongst GAC memberships, that the general functions of 'concentrating the organisation's mind', 'providing a sympathetic sounding board for organisation thinking' and 'clarifying policy' were the most constructive aspects of GAC activities.

It is less evident that the GACs have much power of independent initiative. Some matters have been raised from the floor. At the BBC GAC Sally Oppenheimer MP raised the question of the Time-Life co-productions and Jack Ashley that of hidden microphones used in documentaries. Professor MacGregor braved the embarrassment of the IBA GAC and persisted in discussing the advertising of contraceptives. But when Lord Avebury raised the thorny matter of political parties' time balances on television with Lord Hill, and asked for definitions of political programmes and the period within which balances were maintained he was told that it was 'not in the public interest to divulge the information'.[72]

Neither does it seem that much specific advice is requested of the two GACs. The BBC, it is true, asked about reactions to Ken Russell's film on Strauss and wanted an opinion on the *Yesterday's Men* incident after the rumpus. The IBA GAC was asked to approve the Authority's action in permitting screening of the controversial film about Andy Warhol which it did initially without seeing the film but with two dissentient voices. The BBC's Council was also involved in lengthy consideration of the *Broadcasting in the Seventies* proposals after they had been formulated. Although certain changes are claimed as a result of this debate, it is hard to avoid the feeling that these were more in the nature of planned tactical concessions than of hard won alterations to the original plan.[73]

It would be wrong to leave this subject without mentioning the energy and initiative that is apparent in some of the regional advisory bodies. Smaller, less

45

inhibited by top people, more coherent in outlook, less constricted by lack of time, the BBC's Regional Advisory Committees and the IBA's local radio groups give a hopeful indication of a form of advisory body that may make more sense of advice – in the sense of articulating coherent views of their own – than the larger bodies have succeeded in doing. Regionalism and the disputes surrounding it in broadcasting are a good example of the failure to give proper account to non-metropolitan, non-established minorities. The problem is, a wise regional Chairman observes, that in broadcasting, largely for historical and technical reasons, there is no satisfactory assessment of the sectional case.[74] None the less the responsibility of national broadcasting services to the sectional interest may be critical. Broadcasting in economic recession is a matter of choices rather than opinions. Above all else it is a question of resource allocation rather than programme judgment: education and public service versus entertainment; local versus regional claims on resources; regional versus national claims on resources; amateur versus professional programming; radio versus television. The old questions about 'quality' and 'excellence' and 'taste and violence' as generalities abstracted from any context of decision or action may be less vital in this context of decision making about survival.

In conclusion, both broadcasting organisations claim their advisory bodies as a significant part of their procedures of accountability; by engaging members of the public in the consideration of the national interest in broadcasting, it is true that advisory bodies do indeed involve the energies of many intelligent people. They provide the 'open windows', 'candid friends' and 'sounding boards' needed by broadcasters and they often come up with helpful comment. They serve to crystallise internal thinking and policy. They may even contribute to the self-criticism that Beveridge thought vital. But there is no need to labour the point that self-criticism, and confidential advice as part of the process, is not the same as accountability. These advisory bodies are, in no unkind sense, the creatures of the broadcasting authorities and can operate only at their request. They regard their duty as being 'zealous, but of course not too zealous' in the words of the Chairman of the BBC's General Advisory Council.[75] They comment in general on the practice rather than the principles of broadcasting, exemplified by their close connection with the managerial levels of the broadcasting organisations. Their reports and advice are directed in the case of the BBC to the Executive rather than the Governors. There is nothing wrong with this – indeed, it is a sensible management device – but it has nothing to do with the independent critical initiatives nor the sanctions that are at the heart of accountability. Advisory bodies have of course also always had an important ambassadorial role. But public relations· in this sense are no substitute for open debate and public criticism. The use of PR is at the discretion of the organisation concerned, as logically it must be: accountability and the decisions flowing from it should not.

This returns us to the view expressed in the IBA's evidence to the Annan Committee that advisory bodies have nothing to do with public accountability. Rather, it was suggested, they are an acknowledgement of the rather complicated duty to be seen to be acting properly in seeking to ascertain public opinion on broadcasting matters, and giving the public the impression of having a fair chance of influencing policy. In this sense advisory bodies may be seen as an expression of part of the Authority's duty under Section 24 of the Act to bring the programmes under constant review and ascertain the state of public opinion about them: in that sense literally 'an account presented' of the way in which they have fulfilled this obligation.[76] This is a more subtle point, but again begs the question of whether Section 24 is the sum of the public responsibilities of broadcasting organisations to account for their performances. The Warhol judgment seemed to endorse the view that this is so under present statutes, to the extent that the Authority's only legal obligation is to demonstrate that the required procedures have been followed in exercising its statutory duties.[77] Advisory bodies must then be considered an adjunct of intelligent management rather than a manifestation of Wedell's 'broadly based public control'. To this extent Mrs Warnock and the IBA are to be congratulated for useful service in bringing a rambling debate back to some basis of legal precision.

Other Aspects of Accountability

The main conclusions reached about advisory bodies are broadly speaking applicable to the other aspects of accountability mentioned by broadcasting authorities – research, complaints procedures, information and correspondence. That is to say, that as aspects of the management of broadcasting they can be regarded as means of satisfying the legitimate internal requirements of the organisations they serve. They may also, in the IBA's sense, fulfil legally required procedures. But they cannot answer the need, if such a need exists, for external evaluation of either the operational record or policy goals of broadcasting.

The question of complaints procedures would normally be considered to fall outside the category of accountability as a matter automatically handled by external and independent authorities. It is a matter of surprise – though significant in itself – that the broadcasting authorities have adopted such an adamant line on external complaints bodies and what one would have thought was a comparatively minor concession of autonomy. Research again might be considered an area in which broadcasting authorities could submit their policies to analysis more searching and critical than can be internally provided, without loss of autonomy. James Halloran has suggested:

> Decisions are not made nor are policies formulated in a vacuum. They are subject to the operation of various social, organisational, professional, political and economic forces both inside and outside the broadcasting organisations. These forces could be mapped out by the researcher and the whole broadcasting operation could be located and studied in relation to other institutions within a wider social context . . . We might attempt to answer the following questions: What is the institution's official policy?

What is officially claimed about (its) effectiveness and execution? What is actually being done? What are the effects of this? What are the possible alternatives given existing resources? What wider value considerations should govern the allocation of resources? One of the main tasks . . . is to expand the range of choice by drawing attention to alternative policies. In broadcasting this can be attempted at many levels, from national policy to programme schedules.[78]

This is an economical statement of the goals of accountability, but equally draws attention to the potential of research as an aid to policy formulation. However, as Halloran says: 'Facts can be embarrassing, knowledge can prove unbearable and ignorance can be functional.'[79] The record of the broadcasting organisations in this respect is dismal. Director General Charles Curran has stated roundly that broadcasters 'have no right to pick the pocket of the viewer to find out what is in his head'. He expanded this remark by saying:

The BBC is in the programme-making business and its overriding concern must be with those who make programmes and those who watch and listen to them. We reject the idea that we should contribute to research because it is not part of our proper function to redistribute public money in this way.[80]

This has not of course prevented the BBC from spending large but undisclosed amounts of money on its own broadcasting research in the past, including its vast and inconclusive study of violence in television. Neither has it inhibited the development of sophisticated operational research techniques by the BBC Audience Research Department under Brian Emmett, aimed at maximising 'the gratifications that viewers derive from the services offered'. (Programmes to be measured not only by audience size but in viewer 'grats', a mordant if desperate response to commercial competition from ITV.)[81] This British view of broadcasting, in which socially set goals are subordinated to consumerism and programmes treated as cultural consumer products, was attacked by Kaarle Nordenstreng of the Finnish Broadcasting Company. Questioning Emmett's proposition that the aim of broadcasting organisations was to 'maximise some function which measures the utility of our output to the public', Nordenstreng writes:

The notion of satisfaction seems to imply the gratification of a number of psychological needs, and the utility of the output to the public seems to be a derivative of these gratifications. The whole model is based on how individuals feel about programme output . . . and neglects any broader sociological considerations at the macro level of society. Surely the aims of broadcasting and the evaluation of programme output should not be determined solely in terms of individual receivers. Mass communication necessarily introduces social implications which cannot be tapped by simply looking at the needs of individuals . . . which to a large extent . . . are modified or even produced by the social network in which the individual lives ... Furthermore, a model which is based on the gratifications of individuals is not value-free: inevitably it must work in favour of the *status quo* ... It is by no means the only logical plausible way, and not necessarily the most responsible or democratic.[82]

A similar point in less serious style was made by the Free Communications Group in evidence to the Select Committee on Nationalised Industries when it investigated the ITA.[83] Pointing out that the research budget of the ITA was amalgamated with 'information' in the Accounts, the Group commented that 'it does not seem altogether healthy that supposedly objective research should be so easily confused with what is public relations, even if it is only in the accounts'. After criticising the secrecy of the ITA's research reports and the apparent 'obsession with scheduling and manipulation of audiences to the exclusion of other socially more important areas of research', the submission concluded that 'effective public accountability depends in the end on the public being provided with a constant flow of thorough and detailed information ... on ITV ... and on the full range of options in the future'. This question of access to information is a central one. It is, though, arguably distinct from the task of supplying information to explain and justify actions, which is how the Authorities appear to interpret the role of information in 'relations with the public'. Both broadcasting authorities produce considerable quantities of material about their activities. Formal Reports and Accounts are presented annually to Parliament. The BBC's comes in the form of a handbook of over 350 pages which includes a great deal of additional reference and useful information: the text of the Charter and Licence, a list of Reith lectures, world receiving set ownership, how to get in touch with the BBC and so on. The IBA also produces annual guides to Independent Television and Independent Radio 'designed to interest a wider public than would purchase the Annual Report and Accounts', and in 1976 the BBC followed suit with a popular version of its own Report somewhat unhappily titled *What's Auntie Up To Now?*. The weekly *The Listener* and the IBA's quarterly *Independent Broadcasting* (10,000 free copies distributed) provide additional opportunities for information and discussion of BBC and IBA policies and much of this is excellent. However, on examination the complaint holds true that it lacks critical content and fails to describe or explain the substance of decision-making: that is to say, the results of research, the facts and figures and the various options considered in determining policy.

It is of course arguable that the broadcasting authorities' job is simply to describe what they do, which is produce and broadcast (or supervise the production and broadcasting) of programmes. In their evidence to the Annan Committee the IBA and BBC go out of their way to endorse the Pilkington Committee's classic view on the matter: 'it is ... the programmes which are the test of the authorities' success.' The Report went on to say:

A service of broadcasting should be judged not by the stated aims of the broadcasters but by its achievements; and it is in the light of these achievements that the structure of their organisations should be judged . . . We have considered first the product and then the producer, rather than the reverse.[84]

This sounds almost like common-sense. There are several problems, however. The first is the simple one that the variety and quantity of the 'product' makes it impossible to 'examine' it in its totality, particularly if examination is held to involve viewing and listening, as the IBA insists. The second has been succinctly stated by the television workers in their ACTT Television Commision Report of 1972.[85] Being asked to judge broadcasting organisations by their products, they said, was like being asked to evaluate the role of the Milk Marketing Board by drinking milk: relevant but inadequate. The third is the more complex problem of criteria: how are we supposed to judge the achievements of broadcasting? Pilkington's simplistic formula of 'good broadcasting' is not readily understood except in terms of the criteria applied by professional broadcasters, and:

While Pilkington may suggest that the listeners and viewers are being put first, they are in fact 'the people for whom the service is provided' who are 'interested primarily in what is provided for them'. With the audience relegated to a passive role, the initiative is inevitably shifted back to the broadcasters themselves.[86]

Thus emphasis on programmes as the source of criteria for the judgment of broadcasting actually *erodes* the public role and reinforces the central arbitration role of the professionals. 'On the one hand and on the other but here we stand' is to paraphrase Charles Hill rather crudely,[87] but it has a brute realism echoed in the IBA's dismissal of accountability as a concern 'largely that of a minority'.[88]

There *are* in fact other alternative possible bases for determination of the national interest in broadcasting, though as yet we have no institutions concerned to articulate or present them. As the ACTT report suggested, broadcasting is a process rather than a product, in which case 'What is significant about it is the way in which it contributes to the process of learning and growth in society rather than the professional quality of its individual items'.[89] This might indicate a quite different emphasis on the communicative as opposed to transmissive potential of radio and television. Alternatively, emphasis might be placed on its industrial characteristics and its potential export earnings and employment capacity, or on broadcasting expenditure as a proportion of national spending in comparison with other public services. Or again, as James Halloran has said in his Introduction to the Seminar on Broadcasting Research, quoted above:

Attention (may) have to be given to such matters as comparative social and human costs, and to the optimum use of scare resources at both national and international level. Alienation, participation, the distribution of power and wealth, freedom, dignity, educational opportunities, subsistence levels, housing and health facilities – all are relevant in this connection . . . What constitutes adequate functioning for society as a whole is a question which (we) have been reluctant to ask in the past, but which we must be prepared to ask about every existing media activity and proposed new development.

It is in this perspective of theoretical options that the poverty of information provided about broadcasting by the broadcasting organisations becomes apparent, and its debilitating effect on the level of debate about broadcasting policy a matter for concern. Reference has already been made to the difficulties experienced in getting access to the internal research reports and basic operating figures on which policy decisions are (or should be) based. The IBA is now prepared to publish the franchise applications of successful companies, but still regards its performance reports on ITV and ILR as confidential except for the blandest of summaries. It has never considered (or if it has it has not made public) the implications of the company structure of the ITV companies it supervises, nor commented on the growth of trans-media conglomerates and marketing of programmes. The only detailed account of costs and revenues in ITV appeared in a National Prices and Incomes Board Report in 1970. The BBC has a somewhat similar record, having withheld from publication for a considerable period the McKinsey Management Consultancy Report on its operations and Tom Burns' research study of production teams. The most striking examples are, however, to be found in the absence of financial information. It is remarkable, to say the least, that the two authorities responsible for supervision of expenditure of over £300 million on public service broadcasting should present their accounts in thirteen pages in the case of the BBC (including notes) and ten pages in the case of the IBA (including notes but excluding the details of individual ITV companies, which have to be obtained from company reports). This provides an inadequate basis for informed discussion of existing services, let alone broader consideration of national options in broadcasting.

This, then, is the system held by Wedell to be one of 'extensive and broadly based public control', and described by the BBC as 'a long existing procedure' of public accountability. It is possible to have genuine sympathy with the problems of broadcasters in operating and accounting for complex creative activities and yet be unable to accept these verdicts. Whatever the functions of these aspects of broadcasting administration and supervision – and it is accepted that they have internal values which may be exploited at the discretion of the organisations concerned – their reference is inward, confidential and particular and their public stance, when apparent, largely defensive or ambassadorial. The legal obligation on broadcasting authorities to take advice from General Advisory Councils of 'a broadly representative character' (which is now incorporated in the Charter and Television Act) obscures but does not invalidate Mary Warnock's point about sanctions. Not only is the concept of 'representation' without reference to the interests represented a highly dubious one; but, as has been shown, the operation of the advisory machinery militates in practice against coherent evaluation of current policy and, even more seriously, in assessment of alternatives to that policy. It cannot begin to engage with questions of national interest in broadcasting that encompass both authorities, such as allocation of national resources to broadcasting. (It is of significance that where joint bodies do exist to advise on religious and educational matters, they are more concerned to stake out the ground for diplomatic relationships with other power structures than query the nature of broadcasting's function in these areas.) It is likely that these structural limitations are as definitive as the absence of effective sanctions, but either way the result is the same. There seems no doubt that the IBA's hard line on accountability provides the more accurate description of the realities of power and broadcasting initiative up to this point.

Broadcasting and Parliament

This leaves the crucial final question of whether Governors' and Members' formal accountability to Parliament provides adequate definition and safeguard for the national interest in broadcasting. As has been established by the Court of Appeal's judgment in the Warhol case (McWhirter v. the IBA), in day-to-day management the only legal obligation on the broadcasting authorities is that of being seen to attempt to fulfil their public responsibilities in a reasonable way. 'The Authority were the people who mattered, said His Lordship. They were the censors. The Courts had no right whatsoever and, His Lordship would add, no desire whatsoever, to interfere with their decisions so long as they reached them in accordance with law.' A particularly interesting feature of this judgment was its emphasis on the 'representative and responsible' character of the Members of the Authority and the *fact that they had seen the film.* 'The Court knew that the people who formed the opinion were intelligent and cultured, with a wide range of types of background: the Authority themselves had seen the film.'[90] This at one and the same time disposes of the legal status of editorial independence reserved to broadcasters (confirming the editorial responsibilities of Governors and Members suggested by the *Yesterday's Men* incident), and puts the full onus of responsibility on Governors and Members for accounting to Parliament and the law for the detail of what is done in broadcasting.

There are two main aspects to this parliamentary accountability. In spite of the annual reports presented to them, Members of Parliament in practice have rather restricted opportunities to discuss broadcasting affairs. One occasion occurs during the annual presentation of the broadcasting vote, others in Adjournment Debates, or on the occasion of a Special Motion. The Annual Report and Accounts of the Corporation and the Authority can be discussed when they are submitted to the Minister for presentation to Parliament, if time can be found and if they are not presented during the Parliamentary Recess. The freedom in practice of the two broadcasting Authorities from ministerial direction has meant that Ministers are freed from the liability to defend or discuss the actions of the Authorities in the House of Commons (though the significance of their private interventions may be considerable). It has also meant that parliamentary questions are restricted to the narrow scope of those matters traditionally regarded as being under direct government control – *i.e.* renewals of the Charter and Licence and Television Act, appointments of Governors and Members of the Authority and members of Committees of Enquiry, and questions of frequency allocation. Questions cannot normally be asked in Parliament about programmes, staff appointments or dismissals, salaries, or the expenditure or organisation of the two broadcasting organisations. 'Members', said the Beveridge Report, 'have the same chance as any other members of the public for voicing criticisms and suggestions on broadcasting in the press or on the platform . . . but their opportunities in Parliament are limited. In practice, in its current business, the (broadcasting organisation) is independent of the Government and Parliament . . .'

This leaves the ultimate and indeed only effective power of Parliament over broadcasting in its right to reconsider the structure and disposition of broadcasting organisations. It has done this at fairly regular intervals since the start of broadcasting services in this country, and is empowered to legislate whatever changes it wishes. At this level, as the Beveridge Report pointed out, the ultimate power of the State over broadcasting is absolute. The record of Government Enquiries and their recommendations does not indicate, however, that they have been a particularly effective means of promoting improvements in the system.[92] Few of their suggestions have been adopted, and the major changes such as the introduction of ITV and commercial radio, have been made independently, without reference to Committee investigations. It can be seriously questioned whether these occasional studies by extra-parliamentary bodies, which traditionally have the lesser status of Committees of Enquiry rather than Royal Commissions, are realistically capable of the kinds of investigation relevant to broadcasting and the national interest. This is not so much because of the heterogeneous lay membership of the Committees (though this has been criticised by professionals) nor even because of the absence of adequate research budgets and administrative servicing, but rather because the continuous process of broadcasting and its dynamic industrial and social relationships resist static analysis at given points of time. The Annan Committee, for example, started its deliberations in a period of expansion and technological optimism and concluded them at a time of pessimism and retrenchment. The ultimate effect of this uncertainty is to reinforce the *status quo*.

The final chapter will discuss the implications of this curious state of affairs.

Notes

1. Stuart Hall, 'Broadcasting and Society', an address to ACTT Seminar, September 1971, quoted in ACTT *Television Commission Report*, ACTT 1972.
2. One of the first references to this aspect of broadcasting is to be found in the evidence presented to Annan by the Standing Conference on Broadcasting, which pointed out the relatively high proportion of GNP devoted to broadcasting (including transmission and reception equipment) in the UK as compared with other countries in Europe. This provoked a surprisingly intemperate reaction amongst broadcasters. See Charles Curran's remarks to the Royal Television Society Convention, September 1975: 'Any temptation to think of programme services as "product" and as merely statistical allocations within the Gross National Product is the first step on the road to the degradation of any concept of programme production as a matter of excellence and integrity.'
3. See E. G. Wedell, *Broadcasting and Public Service*, Michael Joseph, 1968, p. 103, on the theoretical emphasis of 'broadly based popular control' in British broadcasting legislation. This chapter will be querying his identification of advisory procedures with mechanisms of control.
4. BBC Evidence to the Committee on the Future of Broadcasting: 'Broadcasting and the Public', BBC 1975, p. 1, para. 3.
5. Talking of the BBC and IBA he said, 'I think that it is useful to describe such bodies not as organs of government – which implies a connection with Ministers and with politics – but . . . as elements in the governance of the country, a formulation which permits one to think of authority without confusing it with politics.' (Address to Royal Television Society Convention, 1975)
6. Symbolically represented by the allocation to the Chairman of the BBC of a small dark room leading off the Director General's suite.
7. A true story from an impeccable source: Hugh Greene as Director General and Sir Arthur Fforde as Chairman went to see R. A. Butler to discuss Fforde's successor. Fforde told Butler: 'You must make sure that whoever you appoint can get on with Hugh.'
8. Colin Shaw, Chief Secretary of the BBC, in an interview with the author in 1973. This procedure was strongly criticised by Pilkington, who said that the DG should not participate (para. 400). The practice apparently continues none the less, though informally. (See above.)
9. In an interview with the author, 1973.
10. Ibid.
11. Sir Peter Scarlett was proposed by the Foreign Office, who wanted an ex-Ambassador on the Board, according to this same official. (See above.)
12. BBC Memorandum: 'The Structure of the Board of Governors', Evidence to the Committee on the Future of Broadcasting, BBC, 1974, p. 6.
13. Governors' duties, composition, etc., are detailed in the BBC Charter, section 5–7; staff in sections 72 and 73.
14. E. G. Wedell, *Broadcasting and Public Policy*, op. cit., p. 114.
15. This question of the amount of time expected from Governors caused embarrassments in the early years of the BBC. Mrs Snowden, one of the first Governors, had been told that her duties were to 'almost fully occupy' her time, and arrived expecting a private office at the BBC. On the other hand Sir Hugh Greene and Sir Learie Constantine rarely attended Governor's meetings in the early seventies.
16. A view of British broadcasting perhaps reflected in the London Chinese Consulate's practice a few years ago of watching only BBC television (Mrs Mary Adams to author).
17. *Report of the Committee on Broadcasting 1960*, HMSO Cmnd. 1735, 1962, para. 408.
18. Ibid., para. 410.
19. In an interview with the author.
20. *Report of the Broadcasting Committee 1949*, op. cit., para. 552.
21. R. Bevins, *The Greasy Pole*, Hodder and Stoughton, 1965, pp. 116–118.
22. Lord Normanbrooke, *The Functions of the BBC's Governors*, BBC, December 1965, p. 11.
23. 'Accountability and Public Service Broadcasting', submission to the Committee on the

Future of Broadcasting, from the Standing Conference on Broadcasting, p. 18. See also Wedell's version of the same view: 'Persons of predominantly middle-class outlook and habits and at the upper end of middle age', Wedell, op. cit., p. 107.

24. Sir Robert Fraser in an interview with the author, 1973.
25. Pilkington *Report*, op. cit., para. 415.
26. See Wedell, op. cit. p. 121.
27. See Professor J. A. G. Griffith's article, 'The Voice of the Consumer', in the *Political Quarterly*, Vol. 21, No. 2, April 1950, for a stimulating discussion of this subject: 'The country is being littered with advisory committees of one sort or another and the standard seems to be declining . . .'
28. Correspondence with the author from a Governor of the BBC.
29. The author's letters to Governors and Members of BBC advisory committees requesting interviews were opened at the BBC and forwarded with a letter 'warning them not to see her', according to one member who was sufficiently annoyed to disregard the advice as a matter of principle. The policy was later changed to one of courteous though wary co-operation. The IBA was more open throughout, though consistently preferring group interviews.
30. Michael Tracey, *The Production of Political Television in Britain*, Routledge and Kegan Paul, 1977, ch. 10; see also his '*Yesterday's Men* – a Case Study in Political Communication' in Curran, Gurevitch and Woollacott (eds.), *Mass Communication and Society*, Edward Arnold, 1977.
31. Michael Tracey: article in *Broadcast*, September 13, 1976.
32. Michael Tracey, ibid.
33. Joe Haines: article in *The Guardian*, July 15, 1971.
34. BBC Memorandum to the Committee on the Future of Broadcasting, 'The Structure of the Board of Governors', para. 3: 'The Board has therefore to be both critic and guardian of the broadcasters.'
35. The Standing Conference on Broadcasting submission, op. cit.
36. Pilkington *Report*, op. cit., para. 418.
37. In an interview with the author.
38. Wedell, op. cit., p. 126.
39. Briggs, op. cit., Vol. II, p. 429.
40. *Report of the Committee on Broadcasting 1949*, HMSO Cmnd. 8116, paras. 552–555 and 557.
41. Pilkington *Report*, op. cit., para. 405.
42. Sir Hugh Greene in an unpublished interview for Joan Bakewell and Nicholas Garnham, *The New Priesthood*, Allen Lane, 1970.
43. Sir Michael Swann speaking to the Royal Television Society Conference, Cambridge, September 1973.
44. Stephen Murphy at ACTT Seminar September 1971, quoted in the ACTT *Television Commission Report*, op. cit., p. 23.
45. Pilkington *Report*, op. cit., para. 426.
46. *E.g.*, Sir Michael Swann's apology to several MPs after an unruly programme, *The People Talking*, in July 1974.
47. See Wedell's useful analysis, op. cit., pp. 110–132.
48. See Reith's comments on Whitley as Chairman quoted by Briggs, op. cit., Vol. II, pp. 430–431.
49. 'A yet sharper criticism of the Authority implied that it had misconceived its relationship with the programme contractors; that it saw itself as advocate for them; that it excused and defended them. The Authority told us that it saw its relationships with the contractors as one between friends and partners. It is our view that, while there is everything to be said for persuasion so long as it is effective, the relationships between the Authority and the companies must be that between principle and agents. As the trustee for the public interest, the Authority is answerable. It must therefore be master, and be seen to be master.' Pilkington *Report*, op. cit., para. 572.
50. Wedell, op. cit., p. 103. See also his interesting comments, pp. 211–212.
51. See Sydney and Beatrice Webb, *Constitution for a Socialist Commonwealth of Great Britain*, Longmans Green, 1920.

52. Internal BBC Memorandum on the Future of the General Advisory Committee, Spring 1937, quoted by Briggs, op. cit., Vol. II, p. 471.
53. *Report of the Broadcasting Committee 1935*, HMSO Cmnd. 5091, para. 46.
54. Ibid., para. 46.
55. Beveridge *Report*, op. cit., para. 562.
56. Ibid., ch. 21.
57. Lord Simon of Wythenshawe, *The BBC from Within*, Gollancz, 1953, p. 71.
58. See Briggs, op. cit., Vol. II, p. 467 for chapter on early development of advisory bodies significantly entitled 'Public Images'.
59. BBC Memorandum 'The BBC and the Public', para. 30, p. 9. Evidence to the Committee on the Future of Broadcasting, BBC, 1975.
60. Ibid., p. 9, para. 31.
61. See John Scupham, *Broadcasting and the Community*, Watts, 1967.
62. 'Communication with the Public', IBA Chairman's statement to Minister, January 1974, included as Appendix XIV in *IBA Annual Report and Accounts*, 1973–74,
63. The Television Act 1964, ch. 21, HMSO.
64. Senior officers of the IBA in conversation with the author.
65. IBA Evidence to the Committee on the Future of Broadcasting, paras. 212 and 213.
66. Lord Aldington, *Advising the BBC*, BBC Lunchtime Lecture, 9th series, No. 3, 1974, p. 13.
67. Lord Avebury, Dame Margaret Miles, Professor Roy Shaw, Theo Crosby in interviews with the author during 1973 and 1974.
68. Memorandum from the BBC General Advisory Council to the Committee on the Future of Broadcasting, para. 28.
69. Second Report from the Select Committee on Nationalised Industries 1971/1972, Sub-Committee B: 'The IBA', HMSO House of Commons Paper 465. If its criticism of inaccessibility is valid, it certainly applies with equal force to the BBC. In response to a letter from the author requesting an interview, a member of the BBC GAC replied:
    'If you are really seeking an interview on the general subject of advisory committees of public and semi-public bodies, I must point out that this is a matter within the scope of my professional practice as a consultant. But I gather from my colleagues that you are really concerned with the adequacy of the GAC as representing the views of the public; and possibly you have already made up your mind and do not need any more interviews. In any event I should regard the advice I personally tender to the Corporation as confidential, but no doubt other members have said the same. I think that what you appear to be investigating is a pretty complex management problem and not primarily political at all; and possibly this does not fit in with your approach . . .'
70. Interview with the author.
71. Member of BBC GAC in interview with author.
72. Interview with Lord Avebury by author.
73. Proposals from the GAC and the Regional Advisory Councils led to modification of the regional networking plans and to the appointment of a Controller, English Regions. See Memorandum from the BBC General Advisory Council to the Committee on the Future of Broadcasting, p. 11.
74. Louis Allen in interview with author.
75. Lord Aldington, *Advising the BBC*, op. cit., p. 5.
76. For further reading on this tortuous argument, try going back to Chapter 5, 'Relations with the Public', in the IBA evidence to the Annan Committee.
77. See McWhirter v. IBA, *The Times* Law Reports, January 16, 26, 29 and February 5, 1973.
78. J. D. Halloran, Introduction to Seminar Report 'Broadcaster/Researcher Co-operation in Mass Communication Research', University of Leicester, 1970.
79. Ibid., p. 19.
80. Ibid., p. 58.
81. Brian Emmett, *Public Opinion Quarterly*, Winter 1968–69. I am indebted to Brian Groombridge, *Television and the People* (Penguin Education Special, 1972) for this and the following reference.

82. Kaarle Nordenstreng, 'Comments on Gratification Research in Broadcasting', *Public Opinion Quarterly*, Spring 1970.
83. 'The ITA's Research Function', Appendix 18, a Memorandum submitted by the Free Communications Group. Second Report of the Select Committee on Nationalised Industries, op. cit.
84. Pilkington *Report*, op. cit., para. 34.
85. ACTT *Television Commission Report*, op. cit., p. 3.
86. Ibid., p. 2.
87. Charles Hill, Foreword to BBC *Handbook*, 1972.
88. IBA Evidence to the Committee on the Future of Broadcasting, para. 203.
89. ACTT *Television Commission Report*, op. cit., p. 2.
90. Court of Appeal judgment in McWhirter v. IBA. See *The Times* 'Law Report', February 5, 1973.
91. Beveridge *Report*, op. cit., paras. 32 and 33.
92. See Sir Hugh Greene, *Third Floor Front*, for his notes on preparation for Pilkington: 'I approached this event as an exercise in psychological warfare: define one's objectives, rally one's friends, rattle one's enemies, and state one's case with the utmost conviction, persuasion and clarity.'

4   The Case for Accountability

The purpose of this study has been to examine the twin concepts of independence and accountability in public service broadcasting. What has this short march through the institutions of British broadcasting established?

Firstly, that as a matter of historical record neither of the two key ideas in the current broadcasting debate – that is to say, broadcasters' independence and public accountability – figured in the original legislative discussion in anything remotely like their present meanings. 'Independence' in the day-to-day management of broadcasting was a matter of informal practical convenience to the Ministry and of efficiency to Reith and the proponents of the public corporation from both right and left. 'Accountability' was firmly and unequivocally to the State through Parliament and the Government of the day. The simplicity and consistency of this approach was based, of course, on confidence in a common view of the national interest in broadcasting at the time. Not for the first time this turned out to be a convenient marriage of moral uplift and commercial expansion.

Secondly, that as a matter of practical experience it turns out that the machinery of public accountability or public relationships described by the Authorities does not work in the full sense – and I think Mrs Warnock's[1] point is correct – of combining both information and sanctions; that is to say, both the right to know about performance of duty and the right to change performer or possibly duty if the performance is judged unsatisfactory. All the advisory machinery described by the BBC as part of its system of public accountability fails to qualify as such in the terms of this definition; it is good management probably, excellent public relations possibly, and socially useful in other ways perhaps, but a red herring as far as the crucial questions of evaluation and change are concerned. (It is not even necessary to pursue the subsidiary argument about the role of these activities in co-opting and using influential sectors of opinion to reinforce the central structures of power in the organisation, though this aspect of their function has long been recognised.)[2] This leaves us with the IBA's altogether tougher and more convincing proposal that 'accountability to the public' does not exist and that the accountability of the broadcasting authorities is only to Parliament.

The shortcomings of parliamentary accountability in the real terms of access to information and opportunities for discussion have already been briefly discussed in the last chapter. (It is interesting that neither the IBA nor Mrs Warnock seem to have evinced any very sympathetic understanding of *why* people have been getting steamed up about public accountability; to demonstrate that a system legally exists is not, after all, to demonstrate that it is satisfactory.) But the central problem of parliamentary accountability lies not in the practical problems of parliamentary procedure, important as they are, but in the thorny question of the independence of the broadcasters. The previously quoted passage from IBA evidence to the Annan Committee is worth repetition because it admirably sets out the heart of the dilemma:

> If the demand is for extra supervision rather than extra information, a problem arises. There is only one organisation, apart from a further supervisory body rather like the Authority itself and duplicating its functions, which could have this task: and that is Parliament, to which the broadcasters are already accountable. Yet Parliament is reluctant itself to require greater accountability from the broadcasters. There would indeed be difficulties were it to do so, difficulties which would worry just those people who advocate more accountability. Parliament has always prided itself on the fact that it does not control, or even interfere in, broadcasting: the ambiguities of 'accountability' are such that it is difficult to separate demands for accountability to be increased from the likelihood that both control and interference would be increased also. It may be for this reason that the emphasis of the discussion has shifted towards 'public accountability' with the implication that accountability to the public can be exercised somehow more directly than by accounting to its elected representatives.
>
> It does not seem to us that the elected representatives can be by-passed in this way, or that they would wish to substitute their own judgment on individual cases for that of the Members whom the Government appoints. For the Members of the Authority are the means by which Independent Broadcasting is responsible to the public without being answerable to its rulers in a way which would weaken the independence from Government which broadcasting, like the press, has in our society.[3]

As we have seen, this is a case that has been developed by broadcasters over the years with increasing emphasis and it is generally accepted as constituting an important element in the conduct of British broadcasting (though interestingly enough the BBC has been prepared to admit that it is not necessarily appropriate in other circumstances in developing nations).[4] Here, however, the idea of broadcasters' freedom is elevated to a position of such absolute and over-riding importance that it takes precedence over all others, including the idea of democratic assessment of the social aspects of broadcasting policy. The final sections of this study will be examining the results that follow from this effective emasculation of parliamentary accountability, and arguing strongly for initiatives to redress the balance in favour of democracy and national, as opposed to broadcasting organisations', interest.

The Collapse of Consensus

What we have now is basically the original legislative structure applied to drastically changed circumstances. The changes are well enough known. The most obvious is the physical growth which has transformed cottage industry radio into the industrial empires of broadcasting which spend hundreds of millions, employ hundreds of thousands, trade throughout the world and link with the massive international conglomerates of the advertising, leisure and telecommunications businesses. For all that broadcasters may like to retain the vocabulary of a mythical Arcadia where all is Delight, Excellence, Integrity and Freedom of Creativity in programming, the world in which they are licensed to pursue these objectives is undeniably ruled by harsher determinants.[5]

Equally important are the complementary changes that have taken place in our perception of mass communication as a force in society capable of wielding, at one and the same time, cohesive and disintegrating influences which resist coherent analysis. Broadcasting is both popular and powerful, as Brian Groombridge points out, 'not only in the sense that the great majority of the population use it and devote most of their spare time to it, but also in the related sense that they like it and trust it'.[6] But it is precisely this popularity and the implication of a further power derived from near universal coverage in the UK that arouses widespread anxiety. The anxiety surfaces in many different forms, ranging from explicit concern about violence and sex in programmes, the effects of viewing on children, and bias in news and current affairs, to demands for better access, participation and accountability embodying implicit criticism of the conduct of broadcasting. (Stuart Hall's figure of the prism perceptively draws attention to broadcasting's special capacity to attract and then split contemporary discontents into a spectrum of conflicting attitudes.) However, what is most striking is not the volume or range of the anxieties, but rather the expression of underlying doubt in the very determination and disposition of authority on which broadcasting in this country is based. As the Annan Committee noted, rightly setting the change of climate in an international and historical context:

> The questions which the public were asking about broadcasting were vastly different from those which concerned the (Pilkington) Committee. They were more critical, more hostile, more political . . . [and included] . . . demands that we should re-examine the whole structure of broadcasting and the political assumptions on which the British system rests. Fifteen years ago people would have found this astonishing.[7]

The effect of these changes? To challenge and then to destroy the basis of consensus on which the original legislation was based. And the effect of this destruction? To corrupt the logic on which the original bargain between broadcasters and the State was constructed. It is important to note that this destruction and corruption are not necessarily dependent on the quality or validity of the criticisms that may be made, and that they follow inevitably from the breakdown of agreement on interpretation of national interest in this area of activity. The broadcasters may decline to heave to – Annan's phrase –

but the well-known strategy of juxtaposing views from right and left to demonstrate that they are on the right course has become an irrelevance. Thus, if we conclude that the evidence suggests no effective machinery of extra-parliamentary accountability to the public, the carefully balanced structure of public service in the hands of independent trustees formally and only responsible to Parliament is upset. The original understanding was formed on the basis of an agreed national interest – in effect an extra-political national interest – that was not seen to involve discussion of major policy disagreements or to require more than negative checks of its conduct. The fact that this understanding of agreed national interest was based on a misunderstanding of the potential of broadcasting does not alter the fact that consensus was the condition on which independence in day-to-day management was granted to the broadcasting authorities. On these grounds alone it can be argued that the bargain requires renegotiation.

But an even more cogent argument can be based on the evolution of broadcasting itself. Quite simply, decisions about broadcasting policy and practice extend far beyond 'the progress of science and the harmonies of art' to involve much wider matters of public concern in almost all areas of public policy. Here, three particular structural problems give grounds for concern. Firstly, the economic power and complexity of broadcasting organisations has increased to an extent that sets in doubt the capacity of part-time trustees to obtain adequate information and to supervise them effectively – Beveridge's point. The infamous Whitley document take-over of Governors by the BBC professionals may have been rejected,[8] but the *Yesterday's Men* incident demonstrates the validity of Wedell's[9] comments about the difficulties of detachment from and indeed the inevitability of complicity of 'amateur' Governors in the affairs of the huge organisation they are supposed to supervise.[10] Similarly, although there are some clear advantages in the administrative separation of the IBA from the commercial companies, its record on advertising[11] and the Levy[12] – and indeed its new Chairperson's somewhat uncritical support for ITV2 in the context of a continuing public debate – indicate that it has not found it easy to separate issues of national interest from the material interests of the companies on whose viability it depends for its own income. The Warhol judgment[13] has confirmed that under the law as it stands such decisions cannot be questioned on other than procedural grounds; that is to say, that the definition of national interest in broadcasting legally rests unequivocally in the hands of authorities intimately involved with the interests of separate and competing organisations.

Secondly, a variety of other organisations and industries are now associated with broadcasting in one way or another, either through direct financial and commercial association with the broadcasting companies and their diversified business interests, or through the international marketing of programme materials or through telecommunications and equipment industries.[14] (It is often forgotten that domestic equipment costs represent the major public investment in broadcasting.) The Post Office, for example, now a profit-making public corporation in its own right, is busily pursuing objectives in the strategic area of telecommunications that will directly effect the economic and social base of public service broadcasting. The point is simply that the national interest in broadcasting cannot reasonably be determined without taking account of these developments, and that the present allocation of authority makes this virtually impossible.

Finally, national objectives potentially involve choices that overlap the boundaries of the two broadcasting authorities: coherent evaluation and decisions about the relative importance of, say, choice in programming; or the role of educational radio and television; or the quantity and sources of finance for broadcasting and the proportion of national resources that they should properly represent, let alone the relatively simple matters of duplicated coverage of major events and a comprehensive programme magazine. Issues of this sort present major problems within the present structure though they are arguably relevant to the national interest in this public service.

These are some of the reasons why British broadcasting policies in the seventies are characterised by stasis, uncertainty and waste. Of course, there are some excellent programmes. So there should be – Britain as a nation is still spending over 1.5% of the GNP on its broadcasting according to a recent estimate, a higher proportion than most other European countries. But we have a ramshackle structure of local radio – 'a mess', says Annan, 'built from the bricks which have been dropped over the past twenty-five or fifty years',[15] though it remains unclear whether the Annan proposals for the finance of the new LBA (Local Broadcasting Authority) are going to set it on a firmer foundation. We have continuing confusion over the allocation of the Fourth Channel, broadcasting's unidentified flying object, occasionally sighted hovering at a considerable height above the earth before disappearing in a puff of smoke. Expensive and persistent uncertainties about the role and character of educational broadcasting remain. There is no clear idea of the desirable patterns of technical development in the broadcasting industry of the future.[16] Most important of all there has been an almost total failure to engage the social potential of radio and television in communal processes of learning, participation and growth, as the absence of coherent examination of parliamentary legislation[17] or any attempt to use television for public health education on a regular basis bear witness.[18] Kaarle Nordenstreng has remarked that 'the aims of broadcasting and the evaluation of programme output should not be determined solely in terms of individual receivers'.[19] This applies with equal validity to individual broadcasting organisations, as members of the film and television union (ACTT) were amongst the first to point out.[20]

Annan and after

The Report of the most recent committee of inquiry into broadcasting (the Committee on the Future of Broadcasting under the Chairmanship of Lord Annan)[21] is of particular interest as the first to consider fundamental criticism of the British system of broadcasting. The main discussion of accountability and the relationships of public, broadcasters and State is contained in Chapters 4, 5 and 6 of Section 11 'Foundations for the Future'. An urbane but orthodox approach to these troublesome topics is, however, firmly established in Chapter 3 which unequivocally endorses the Pilkington emphasis on programmes as the test of broadcasting systems; programmes, moreover, which, it claims, it is one of the achievements of British broadcasting to regard as 'hand-made products produced by individual craftsmen and not as articles of mass production':

> We do not agree with those who have suggested that the concern of the Pilkington Committee for good programmes was somehow misconceived and that the real issue is the control of broadcasting. The contention that the overweening power of the broadcasters who 'set the agenda' and 'define reality' for the public and 'structure the view between governors and governed' must be curbed, while at the same time the individual producer is to be granted far greater freedom, seems to us a mysterious paradox . . . We regard the programmes as unquestionably the most important – and arguably the only – test of any broadcasting system. And so, we think, do the public. Any broadcasting system must be judged by the quality of its programmes (para. 323).

Chapter 4 then proceeds to analyse the four requisites for good broadcasting which are defined as flexibility, diversity, editorial independence and accountability. Discussion of the last two recognises the conflict between demands for more freedom for the broadcasters and greater accountability to the public, but concludes that this can be best resolved – indeed only resolved – through the traditional formula of trustees of the public interest, the Governors and Members who must 'inescapably resemble Janus'. The detail of the argument is of considerable interest, as much for its omissions as for its sharp observations. (The section on accountability, for example, has a factual account of the machinery of parliamentary accountability in Para 4.13 but no discussion of the effectiveness of the arrangements or of the value of the ultimate sanction of dismissal, surely a question of crucial interest.)

This section is immediately followed by an attack on the various proposals for an Executive Broadcasting Commission submitted to the Committee. The grounds of objection to such a proposal are that it would 'lead to one body of people being able to impose their views on the whole of broadcasting output'; that it would increase the risk of political control over broadcasting; and that it would lead to 'rigidity, limitation of choice, a threat to freedom of expression, of political interference, and spreading bureaucratisation' (Para. 4.21). In a remarkable passage the Report continues (my emphasis):

> There is the danger that a Broadcasting Commission . . . would spawn a substantial and power-hungry secretariat, all the more dangerous because not firmly under ministerial control and all the more confusing because liable to usurp what are strictly speaking the functions of the Secretary of

State and his civil servant advisers . . . It would be all the more dangerous because although theoretically responsible it would, unlike the Broadcasting Authorities or the Government, be irresponsible in practice . . . Both Government and Broadcasting Authorities have to look to the public – *either as an electorate or as an audience – and fear its displeasure expressed in election results or poor ratings.* A Commission would not be directly and continuously responsible in this sense (Para. 4.21).

Programmes are made by people who create them, and creation does not express itself through the rational application of rules, guide-lines or regulations (Para. 4.23).

The Committee chooses the words of the Institute of Practitioners in Advertising to conclude that a single Authority on the lines of a Broadcasting Commission would be either 'redundant, or too powerful to be socially desirable'.

In dealing with the role of the Broadcasting Authority in general the Report describes the Members and Governors as:

Guardians of the public interest, and as such bound at times to intervene, chide or even discipline the broadcasters in the public interest. Yet at the same time and equally in the public interest they must stand up for the broadcasters' independence and defend them if they consider that in controversy with the Government or with pressure groups of one sort or another, the broadcasters are in the right (Para. 4.27).

Their job is to 'censure not censor', and they must be able to 'take broadcasters by the elbow rather than twist their arm'.

In the end someone has to have the responsibility for deciding which aspect of the public interest should prevail, and what can be broadcast in particular circumstances at any given time. In our view the ultimate responsibility should rest with the Authorities, as the mediators between the professional broadcasters and the public. The Authorities are themselves accountable to Parliament for their decisions, and Parliament itself is accountable to the electorate. This pragmatic solution to a complex problem has stood the test of fifty years operation and we consider should be maintained in its essentials (Para. 4.31).

The other chapters of the Report which are directly relevant to the questions of independence and accountability are those dealing with the *Powers of Government and the Responsibilities of Parliament* (Chapter 5); and *Broadcasting and the Public* (Chapter 6). Following the conclusions of the previous sections, the Report recommends that Government powers should remain the same, including present powers on financial matters. 'They enable the Government to exercise general control in the national interest over the total financial resources available for broadcasting but not to intervene in the day-to-day management of broadcasting services and in particular, not to regulate expenditure on programmes.' (Para. 5.6) Governors and Members should be paid more, and their selection should be (in one of Annan's better quips) from amongst the Lesser and Better as well as the Great and the Good. The relations between Government and Parliament and the Broadcasting Authorities, the Committee concludes, 'do not require much adjustment'. Where the relations between broadcasters and the public are considered unsatisfactory, the Committee suggests the creation of a joint Broadcasting Complaints Commission, rejects the proposals for a Broadcasting Council or an independent broadcasting Policy Research Centre, and finally backs a dark horse in the shape of a Public Enquiry Board (Para. 6.30–6.37), which is to carry out septennial investigations, 'to take a general view of broadcasting in the public interest'.

This seems to me to be a disappointing analysis, though in its way an accurate illustration of the debilitated condition of the British communications debate. Item: no qualification of the loaded vocabulary of traditional discussion – 'interference', 'meddling', 'bureaucratisation' and 'political pressure'. Item: no examination of the nature of broadcasters' freedom within the context of a competitive industry. Item: no organised investigation of investment, diversification of ITV companies, the concentration of media interests, the employment of women and minority groups or the import and export of programme material, among many other matters relevant to the future of broadcasting that depend on fact rather than opinion. Item (predictably): loss of nerve at the point when identified flaws have to be related to deeper diagnosis of structural deficiencies.[22]

An interesting passage in the conclusions of the Report exemplifies the superficial stylistic strengths and the more fundamental analytical weaknesses of this approach:

There has already been some public debate about how the BBC and IBA could reform their advisory bodies so as to involve some of those members of the public who want their advice to be heard. Our Report is intended to freshen that debate. We have been urged to make sizeable extensions to the bureaucracy of broadcasting. We do not propose that a body similar to ourselves should sit in perpetuity. The credibility of Committees such as ours depends on their being auto-destructs; after orbiting in space they disappear when they report, and their recommendations are motivated only by a desire to do what is best for broadcasting and not to provide themselves with more tasks for permanent employment or jobs for dependents. We were urged to recommend that Commissions or Councils should be set up above the Authorities. We have not done so. We are not in favour of new bodies designed to lay down new rules and regulations and either lord it over the Authorities or continuously lavish them with advice. The Authorities are there to act in the public interest. Let them act. We prefer editorial independence tempered by the recognition that mistakes in taste or policy should be frankly and openly acknowledged by those responsible.

Pennies and pounds should be put into programmes not into policing them (Para. 30.8).

Now it would be unwise to accept the *faux naïveté* of this carefully calculated text entirely at face value since the 174 recommendations that follow it include proposals for the creation of four major bodies (Local Broadcasting Authority, Open Broadcasting Authority, Public Inquiry Board and Telecommunications Advisory Board) that would tend, at the very least, to increase the costs, jobs and sources of advice that are considered superfluous. The plain man's view of bureaucracy, admirable as far as it goes, is simply inadequate as a response to the complex arguments about accountability in public service. Of course it is undesirable that official committees create jobs for themselves or their dependents, or recommend new bodies just for their own sake. This is, however, a necessary condition of their operation rather than a primary objective, and it is the objectives of the Committees that are at the crux of the matter.

The objective of a Committee of Inquiry into Broadcasting is the disinterested critical consideration of the public service provided and of its future development, a task that has been widely regarded, as we have seen, as the keystone of the system of accountability that safeguards the national stake in broadcasting. But does this, or does this not, include the definition – and if necessary redefinition – of the national interest in broadcasting itself? If it does not, then the committee's work is reduced to that of an occasional programme review, to which it can apply what are essentially professional criteria; or, alternatively, it can set itself up as the spokesman of consumer standards, in which case it becomes something like the Tribunal of Taste rejected by Annan. A glance at previous Committee Reports indicates that none has wished to define its role so narrowly. But if it *does* include definition of the national interest, then it is precisely the difficulties of concern without responsibility and advice without authority – difficulties accurately discerned by the Annan Committee – that undermine confidence in any Committee's capacity to fulfil this brief. As the Broadcasting Authorities have themselves broadly hinted from time to time, why should we imagine that an unrepresentative and occasional lay committee which has described itself as orbiting in space before auto-destruction should be able to reach 'better' conclusions about the national interest than those of the authorities that have professional experience of the broadcasting service and statutory responsibility for its conduct in that interest? It is highly significant that the proposals of previous Committees, the last three at any rate, have in retrospect played so marginal a role in the development of broadcasting institutions in this country. Without prejudice to its several pertinent insights, it looks probable that the Annan Report's major recommendations will join them in the footnotes to future generations of media study research papers. The reason, I believe, is that these committees are without political authority. While they undoubtedly enrich the public debate, there is ultimately no way of defining national interest in a democratic society in abstraction from the political process.

Public Interest versus National Interest

It is in the context of this dilemma that the now common substitution of the concept of 'public interest' for the original idea of 'national interest' (a practice endorsed by Annan) acquires a particular importance. What the new usage reflects, I think, is a diversion from those determinants of broadcasting central to the conduct of public service – that is to say, finance, the definition of objectives and the choice of strategic options – towards the more diffuse particulars of programming and its effects.[23] This is registered in the famous Pilkington definition of public interest in broadcasting:

> The Governors' and Members' concern is to represent and secure the public interest in broadcasting. It is for them to judge what the public interest is, and it is for this that they are answerable. They must not do so by assessing the balance of opinion on this or that element of programme content and then adopting the majority view for their own; for . . . this would be to mistake 'what the public wants' for the public interest. Their task is to be thoroughly aware of public opinion in all its variety, to care about it and take proper and full account of it. Having done so they must then identify the public interest in broadcasting, defined as the fullest realisation of the purposes of broadcasting, and secure it through the executive arm.[24]

To be fair to Pilkington, this formulation was only part of an extended argument demonstrating that commercial criteria were incompatible with the fullest possible realisation of the purposes of broadcasting. In the event, however, it has provided broadcasters with a potent ideological weapon which they have been swift to exploit. By 1977 the IBA had the gall to describe commercial television as 'a significant democratic development'[25] and the confidence is echoed in statements by senior broadcasting spokesmen. Huw Wheldon of the BBC, for example, says:

> The essential relationship is between the subscriber (who) makes the licence payments and the broadcasters who use that money to make programmes. What is good about these arrangements is that they make us take the audience very seriously. They pay. And they pay directly.[26]

Lord Hill on the same theme says:

> Who are the communicators responsible to? First and foremost, I suggest, to the public. In the last resort it is the people, the nation, who have granted us our freedom. They are also the people to whom we are communicating. Our service to the community, then, is our paramount responsibility.[27]

What these opinions have in common is a claim to an extra-political power

67

base and, implicitly, to a legitimation forged in the market place and independent of Parliament. And the danger of this lies not so much in its gross misrepresentation of the historical development of the licence fee or the one-way transaction with the publics to whom broadcasting is distributed, as in its challenge to the status and structures of democratic political decision. (The true character of the relationship is effectively demonstrated in the BBC boast that it received more correspondence about a single change in the radio serial *The Archers* than all serious criticism of other programmes put together.)[28] The risk of this populist formulation is in the way that it is currently used to extend the important but particular argument about political manipulation of programmes. What a White Paper described correctly as 'the need to remove from the party in power the temptation to use the State's control of broadcasting for its own political ends'[29] becomes a justification for removing broadcasting organisations from all parliamentary constraints and direction. In the IBA's memorable phrase, broadcasters prefer to be 'responsible to the public without being answerable to its rulers'.[30] Or, as Charles Curran put it, to describe themselves 'not as organs of Government which implies a connection with Ministers and with politics, but as elements in the governance of the country, a formulation which permits one to think of authority without confusing it with politics'.[31]

In the face of this drift towards the interest of powerful oligarchies – and oligarchies which, it must be noted, are increasingly concerned with their international trading and investment in telecommunication and leisure industries – there is much to be said for the idea of a national interest in broadcasting. The reasons are simple but worth restating.

First, broadcasting involves the disposition of limited national resources (public funds, broadcasting frequencies). There is a unitary national interest in the disposition of these resources and a real sense in which the choices cannot be devolved to more than one independent authority. This point was not sufficiently realised when the BBC monopoly was broken.

Second, it has always been recognised that there is a unitary national interest in the social implications of broadcasting. Originally this could be defined in the simple terms, say, of national coverage and moral uplift. Unanimity in the definition and desirability of these two objectives is now eroded and new areas of controversy have emerged (for example the use of broadcasting for public service announcements, or by political parties); but this suggests a greater rather than a reduced need for the discussion and formulation of national policy objectives. Again, it is difficult to see how these policy decisions can be satisfactorily reached on an *ad hoc* basis by separate institutions. It can be added that the immense pressures for expansion in the telecommunications field that are already apparent make it highly desirable that there is a coherent evaluation and expression of social needs and national priorities capable of resisting the pressures if necessary.

Third, a public service must be responsive to changes in public needs. Precisely because the national interest in broadcasting is a dynamic rather than a static concept it must be continuously under examination so that necessary changes can be brought about. And because these changes may on occasion conflict with the self-interest of a broadcasting authority, their determination cannot be devolved to such an authority.

Fourth, the essence of public service in a democratic society is democratic accountability and accountability cannot be fudged. Accountability is the right to know and the power to change. It is not substitutable by 'responsibility' or by 'consultation and advice'. It is not adequately expressed in ratings, market research by commercial companies or programme correspondence with the BBC. If there is a national interest in broadcasting in any of the terms described above it makes sense that the rights of ultimate parliamentary control over the public service be jealously maintained and reinvigorated; maintained not for the purpose, as is sometimes suggested, of harrassing professionals in their day-to-day business or lavishing them with advice, but to reinstate the collective interest in the fullest realisation of the potential of broadcasting which we are in imminent danger of losing altogether.

Some Theoretical and Practical Implications

This case study has attempted no more than a brief discussion of the notion of accountability in broadcasting, examining the ways in which its interpretations have responded to changes in the nature and economic context of British broadcasting, and how in turn these interpretations have been reflected in structure and practice over the last fifty years. The changes have been neither consistent nor coherent in any self-conscious sense, but what emerges is a strong evolutionary tendency away from the state control on which the original institutions were founded. This tendency has sought and found ideological support in the concepts of broadcasters' freedom and public service. The notion of accountability has also been increasingly deployed by broadcasting authorities to describe the machinery of advice, consultation and research that they employ, and by implication to legitimise the status of their independent interpretations of the national interest. The study argues that this use of 'accountability' is illegitimate for the straightforward reason that none of these activities involves the right to know and the power to change the policies of the authorities concerned; the bodies concerned are accountable to the authorities rather than the other way round. The study also suggests that the concept of accountability in a public service can only be defined in relation to national interest. This, it is argued, can in turn only be defined in a democratic society through the political process.

There is in conclusion a third and more general observation to be made. While the trend away from state influence has been clearly identified, it can also be seen that broadcasting and its institutions are at the conjunction of a number of conflicting pressures. Although the interests of the broadcasting industry have been dominant, others are still in play. Most important of all, the formal accountability of broadcasting authorities to the State is still intact in terms of the 'right to know and the power to change' definition. What has diminished the exercise of this ultimate parliamentary authority is to a large extent the potent fear of its manipulation by the party in power; but also, I would argue, to an unrecognised degree *the extreme practical difficulties involved.* Parliamentary oversight is restricted, as we have seen, by severe problems of procedure and lack of information created by the traditional ban on discussion of the day-to-day business of broadcasting. The articulation of the national interest in broadcasting by Governors and Members is fatally confused; not only by their inevitable gravitation towards the interests of the industries with which they are most closely associated, but also by more fundamental flaws in the concept of separate and conflicting national interests that their role embodies. Finally, the exercise of ministerial responsibility is dispersed between various Ministries and expressed in legislation designed for the infant radio service of the twenties. This legislation, and indeed the relations between Parliament and public service broadcasting, have never been reconsidered in the light of the growth of the industry and its international connections, or the introduction of ITV in the fifties.

Revival of concern about accountability reflects anxiety about this highly unsatisfactory state of affairs; as indeed the speed with which broadcasting authorities have sought to incorporate the notion in their official doctrine may be taken as indication of the force of the criticism implied. Of course Raymond Williams is right to stress state linkage rather than state dependence as the characteristic of British broadcasting institutions, a point that reaffirms the importance of media industries within the state apparatus as a whole.[32] However, this distinction itself turns very precisely upon the degree to which the industries concerned are accessible to parliamentary intervention. There is a delicate balance between the flows of influence, and the question is in which direction the decisive influence flows. This I have come to believe is the crucial issue around which the debate about accountability in broadcasting revolves. The choice presented is of more than theoretical importance. On the one hand we can opt for the continuing *ad hoc* development of broadcasting institutions, powered by the expansionary pressures of the Post Office and the telecommunications and leisure industries, and policed (I think Annan's word is correct) by existing Government regulations. On the other, we can confront the politicisation of broadcasting issues (no more than a recognition of the breakdown in consensus in broadcasting matters that has already taken place) and set about the rehabilitation of the structures of political accountability in broadcasting that will enable us to articulate coherent objectives, priorities and strategies that define an evolving national interest in broadcasting.

What would be the implications of such an approach? Since 'politicisation' has a demonic ring in the vocabulary of British social discourse, let us start by discussing briefly what it would *not* imply. For a start, it would not imply the introduction of a State propaganda machine or the political manipulation of programmes by the party in power, which would be totally unsympathetic to the climate of public opinion and political reality in this country. One of the serious criticisms of the present organisation of broadcasting in this country is the fact that it allows political pressures while ensuring that they are concealed in the covert and personalised relationships between broadcasters and senior civil servants and politicians.[33] If a more public discussion of broadcasting policy allowed disagreements to be openly expressed rather than privately resolved this would be all to the good. Similarly, if a state propaganda machine were ever to be created again, as it was during the last war, it could only occur as the result of a democratic decision in the face of extreme emergency.

Neither would it imply a 'Hobbes-like state of anarchy', which is, on reflection, a fairly accurate description of the existing authorities' programme policies and the random way in which broadcasting institutions have been assembled over the years. Rather, it should facilitate a more considered approach to programming and to the questions of public importance (cable television, community access, the rights of reply and the Fourth Channel spring to mind) which have been so startlingly bungled within the present system.

It would not mean boring programmes, loss of choice or lack of variety. To the extent that competition between broadcasting authorities at present effectively reduces choice and variety in the pursuit of good ratings, one would expect to see a more flexible use of broadcasting for a wider variety of social purposes. Expression of more varied opinion and minority interests, encouragement of a greater diversity of broadcasting organisations and sources of production, better coverage of matters of public interest, and more imaginative use of resources for public service purposes such as health education are all highly desirable. At present they are restricted by the structures and constraints, largely economic, that determine the policies of the Authorities. While the ultimate quality of individual programmes involves creative judgments that cannot be prescribed, they are also responsive to a number of factors such as scheduling, finance, working conditions, and employment policies and programme strategies that can.

It would not imply proliferation of bureaucracy and interference; rather a simplification of the network of influence and uncertain regulation to which broadcasting is subject at present. It is often forgotten that accountability is designed to reduce bureaucracy, to devolve responsibility and to liberate initiative at all levels. Meddling, heckling, interference and general aggravation are symptoms of the absence of adequate procedures of accountability rather than the reverse.

It would not imply reduction of professional standards. Rather, it should mean that the skills and experience of the men and women working in the industry would be recognised and given a voice in the determination of its policies. It should also mean – and I think that this is wholly desirable – that investment in technology would be closely examined for its public benefits and effects on those working in the industry, and that the application of professional standards would always be considered in relation to the particular local or national conditions that were relevant.

71

Finally, it would not destroy the freedom of the broadcaster in the vital sense of liberty of expression common to all citizens. However, it has to be said that this is a highly artificial principle within broadcasting and is likely to remain so. Broadcasting operates at present within a complex legal framework that sets out a vast body of rules about balance, obscenity, broadcasting hours and many other matters. Beyond that, the fiercely defended but elusive concept of editorial independence is directly subject to the intervention of Governors and Members, IBA staff, and, on occasion, the Chairmen of commercial television companies. Ultimately individual programmes have to be seen as small items in the continuous production flow of very large organisations, the end products of a continuous process of interference, direction and alteration. It is realistic and necessary that we recognise the industrial revolution that has overtaken broadcasting and cease to discuss this issue solely in terms of nineteenth century radical newspapers.

On the positive side, the general argument for the parliamentary accountability of public service broadcasting has already been made. It rests, in summary, on the proposition that a public service must be continuously defined in terms of national objectives and priorities (the national interest) and that these cannot be identified and legitimised except through the political process. In reverse, as it were, this argues that only parliamentary accountability (politicisation) will release the full social potential of broadcasting by concentrating attention on the rational use of resources, the identification of priorities, and the creation where necessary of new forms of broadcasting organisation. There is an inevitable sense of anti-climax when one attempts to translate such grandiose expectations into practical forms, but for what it is worth the concluding paragraphs of this study detail some of the principles and structures that I think might be involved. They are presented with considerable hesitancy. Partly because they are highly summarised and there are certain to be better alternatives and many interesting modifications that I have been insufficiently ingenious to consider. Mostly because the detail of the changes will have to follow from initial acceptance of the principle of politicisation rather than the other way round. This is bound to be controversial, but I believe that the analysis has a logical consistency that does not depend on the acceptability of these particular suggestions. However, since the objective is wider public discussion of the issues as a whole, here they are. I hope, in Annan's words, that they can help to 'freshen that debate'.

A Central Policy Authority

The most urgent need is for a central body to handle those areas in which there is a unitary national interest in broadcasting and to decide to what subsidiary bodies other matters of broadcasting policy and practice can be devolved. The original solution was to create such a body with monopoly control over broadcasting (the BBC) and subject it to the overriding authority of a responsible Minister (The Postmaster General). The logic of that system has been upset both by the creation of a rival authority (the IBA) and by the separation of responsibility between various Ministries (currently the Home Office and the Department of Industry).

One course of action might therefore be to reinstate ministerial responsibility in a new Ministry responsible for both the social and technological aspects of broadcasting. There are several difficulties about this, including the problem of isolating the area of new ministerial responsibility from existing Ministries, the substantial degree of power and independence exercised in practice by the existing broadcasting authorities, and the likelihood that any new Ministry would inherit the personnel and attitudes that have traditionally governed relationships with broadcasters. On balance I am therefore inclined to believe that within British institutional tradition the best solution would be to recreate a separate broadcasting authority on the lines of the present IBA without direct involvement in programme-making but with responsibility for all broadcasting services to Parliament through a designated Minister. The relationship of its Chairman to the Minister would be similar to that of the Chairman of the Board of a nationalised industry – that is to say, not without conflict.

For this reason the composition of such an Authority would be crucial, and it is disappointing that the Annan Report did not give more than superficial attention to the proposals for an innovatory approach to this question. A key feature of a new approach to the membership structure of such an Authority should include statutory representation of different interests and in certain cases the election of representatives by the interests concerned. The interests represented should include political parties, national organisations, local government, the labour movement and broadcasting organisations, plus Ministerial nominees. Although there are considerable problems involved in arriving at an acceptable formula for membership (numbers, pay, full or part-time, tenure and so forth) there are a number of models in existence, notably in Sweden, Canada and the Haut Conseil de L'Audio Visuel in France, which could provide useful experience and guidance.

The responsibilities of this Authority would be primarily the consideration of the finance and structure of broadcasting organisations, together with the preparation of guidelines for the nature of the public service to be provided. Proposals for major changes in the structure of broadcasting organisations would have to be submitted to the Minister for approval by Parliament.

Parliamentary Discussion

As a necessary corollary of the creation of an Authority with these powers and responsibilities, it would seem desirable to revise the traditional ban on parliamentary discussion of the day-to-day management of broadcasting. Although this raises the spectre of obsessive interest in the details of broadcasting which may become a nuisance, it seems to me that it is none the less essential. It is difficult to see how the principles of public service *can* be discussed without reference to the details of day-to-day business, and it is surely not the case that the right to raise matters in the House, already permitted across a wide range of personal and business matters, constitutes political manipulation of programmes. Broadcasting debates would regularly consider the reports of the new Authority.

Variety of Broadcasting Organisations

On the other side of the equation, the creation of the Broadcasting Authority would necessarily involve some diminution of the powers of the existing Broadcasting Authorities. More precisely, if the new Authority were introduced before other major changes in the structure of broadcasting, as it could be, it would involve incorporation of the powers of the IBA and the Governors of the BBC. However, implicit in the proposal for the creation of a new overall Authority is a much more flexible approach to the structure of broadcasting. Given the political will to take a fresh look at broadcasting, it would seem desirable that the new Authority question the financial basis of commercial broadcasting and the organisation of radio and television within the BBC. Once the monolithic presence of the twin organisations is under close examination, scrutiny may suggest a whole new variety of broadcasting organisations, including local radio stations under community control. (I am inclined to be pessimistic about the viability of local television at the community access level, largely for economic reasons.) It is of course vital that the interests of workers in the industry be fully safeguarded in any proposals made, and that the broadcasting unions are involved in the discussion of such proposals at the highest level.

Access to Information

Finally there has to be, as an essential condition of accountability and indeed as a pre-condition of any reform, a radical change in the public right of access to information about broadcasting affairs. It has been one of the public scandals of broadcasting management in this country that the operation of an important public service has been conducted with all the discretion of a high-class house of assignation. This has encouraged the wildest speculation as to what goes on inside, but has severely inhibited intelligent discussion of policy.[34] There are glossy hand-outs readily available, but hard facts on research, finance, investment, frequency allocation, profits or advertising, let alone the opinions of the Governors and the Authority on matters within their competence and concern, are extremely hard to come by. This is an issue that of course extends far beyond the confines of the broadcasting debate. There is now widespread feeling that open government requires that official information which does not threaten the security of the state should be legally accessible. Scandinavia and the United States already possess such legislation guaranteeing citizens access to all such official information unless specifically classified. The essential point about this legislation is that the burden is on government to establish the necessity for secrecy, and that the final arbitration is made by an impartial arbiter such as the courts or an ombudsman. There is urgent need for such legislation in the UK. However, it is essential that if such legislation is introduced it should contain provision for access to the information of all bodies, including commercial companies, where they are involved in the provision of public services or are associated with the activities of public corporations.

Although only a few may originate a policy, we are all able to judge it. We do not look upon discussion as a stumbling block in the way of political action, but as an indispensable preliminary to acting wisely.[35]

Notes

1. Mary Warnock, 'Accountability, Responsibility – or Both?' *Independent Broadcasting*, No. 2, November 1974.
2. See the chapter on advisory bodies in Briggs, op. cit., Vol. II, p. 467: 'Public Images'.
3. IBA Evidence to Committee on Future of Broadcasting, 1974, paras. 205–206.
4. Sir Michael Swann, *The Responsibility of the Governors*, October 1974.
5. For an excellent account of the structure of British broadcasting and other media see Peter Golding, *The Mass Media*, Longmans, 1975.
6. Brian Groombridge, *Television and the People*, Penguin Education Special 1972, p. 221.
7. *Report of the Committee on the Future of Broadcasting* (Annan *Report*), HMSO Cmnd. 6753, 1977, paras. 2.1 and 2.30.
8. *Committee on the Future of Broadcasting 1949* (Beveridge *Report*), HMSO Cmnd. 8116, p. 52.
9. E. G. Wedell, *Broadcasting and Public Policy*, Michael Joseph, 1968, p. 121.
10. See Sir Michael Swann's suggestion that the BBC Governors have 'something of the function of management consultants' made in his lecture: *The Responsibility of the Governors*, op. cit.
11. For example, since 1973 the IBA has used television to publicise the fact that all television commercials are monitored to see that they conform to their code of advertising practice.
12. See *IBA Report and Accounts*, 1970–71.
13. McWhirter v. IBA, *Times* Law Report, February 5, 1971.
14. For the best analysis of the current structure and its implications, see 'For a Political Economy of Mass Communication' by Graham Murdock and Peter Golding in *The Socialist Register 1973*, Merlin Press, 1974.
15. Annan *Report*, op. cit., para. 14.6.
16. Viz. the Annan *Report* discussion of cable transmission and local radio.
17. See the ACTT report *One Week* for the results of a film and television workers' investigation of the coverage of the Industrial Relations Bill in 1971. The author undertook an informal analysis in 1975 of coverage of the Community Land Bill during its progress through Parliament, on behalf of the School for Advanced Urban Studies, University of Bristol, with similar results.
18. See for example an article by Dr Hugh Jolly in *The Times*, July 12, 1977, dealing with problems of health educators in counteracting the effects of heavy advertising and commercial pressures.
19. Kaarle Nordenstreng, *Public Affairs Quarterly*, Spring 1970.
20. ACTT *Television Commission Report*, 1972.
21. *Report of the Committee on the Future of Broadcasting*, HMSO Cmnd. 6753, 1977.
22. See Jeremy Tunstall, 'Annan in Wonderland', *The Media Reporter*, Vol. 1, No. 3, 1977, for a useful critique of the Annan *Report*.
23. The emphasis on participation and access in the course of the debates of the last few years may have had a rather similar effect in distracting attention from the key issue of accountability.

24. Pilkington *Report*, para. 408.
25. IBA evidence to the Annan Committee, para. 34.
26. Huw Wheldon quoted by Charles Curran in 'The Independence of the Broadcaster', Royal Television Society, September 1975.
27. Lord Hill, 'Freedom of the Communicator', BBC, 1968.
28. *BBC Annual Report and Accounts*, 1970–71.
29. White Paper on Broadcasting Policy, 1946, HMSO Cmnd. 6852.
30. IBA evidence to the Annan Committee, para. 206.
31. Charles Curran, speech to Royal Television Society, op. cit.
32. Raymond Williams in introduction to debate on Marxism and the Mass Media, reprinted in *Wedge*, No. 1, Summer 1977.
33. See BBC Memorandum for the Committee on the Future of Broadcasting, part IX: 'The BBC and the public', for descriptions of 'frequent and informal contact' between senior staff and MPS. The 'contacts with other bodies with views on broadcasting' also mentioned have been a traditional and generously interpreted aspect of broadcasting PR. Mrs Mary Adams, a member of staff during the period, has referred to 'visits to Glyndebourne' being part of the pattern of pre-war affluence (interview with the author). Incidental information: the BBC Management Committee were entertaining Conservative Shadow Minister Anthony Barber at the Dorchester when the news of Charles Hill's appointment as Chairman of Governors came through.
34. Professor Dallas Smythe of Simon Fraser University, British Columbia, reported after an international comparative study of broadcasting systems in Albania, China, France, Hungary and Britain that British information was the most difficult to obtain.
35. Pericles, quoted by Karl Popper in *The Open Society and its Enemies*, Routledge and Kegan Paul, 1957 edn.

Select Bibliography

Key Sources

Annual Report and Accounts of the British Broadcasting Corporation.
Annual Report and Accounts of the Independent Broadcasting Authority.
BBC Memoranda to the Committee on the Future of Broadcasting 74.
IBA Evidence to the Committee on the Future of Broadcasting 74.
Broadcasting Committee Report (Sykes Committee), HMSO Cmnd. 1951, 1923.
Report of the Broadcasting Committee (Crawford Committee), HMSO Cmnd. 2599, 1925.
Report of the Broadcasting Committee (Ullswater Committee), HMSO Cmnd. 5091, 1936.
Report of the Broadcasting Committee 1949 (Beveridge Committee), HMSO Cmnd. 8116, 1951.
Report of the Broadcasting Committee 1960 (Pilkington Committee), HMSO Cmnd. 1753, 1962.
Report of the Committee on the Future of Broadcasting (Annan Committee), HMSO Cmnd. 6753, 1977.
Second Report from the Select Committee on Nationalised Industries, Session 1971–72, sub-committee B. HMSO House of Commons paper 465.

The Development of British Broadcasting

Asa Briggs, *The History of Broadcasting in the United Kingdom*, OUP, 3 Vols., 1965.
D. N. Chester, 'Management and Accountability in Nationalised Industries', *Public Administration*, Spring 1952.
R. H. Coase, *British Broadcasting: A Study in Monopoly*, Longmans, 1958.
Peter Golding, *The Mass Media*, Longmans, 1975.
Peter Golding and Graham Murdoch, 'For a Political Economy of Mass Communication', *Socialist Register 1973*, Merlin Press.
Lincoln Gordon, *The Public Corporation in Great Britain*, OUP, 1938.
A. H. Hanson (ed.), *Nationalisation, A Book of Readings*, Allen and Unwin, 1963.
W. A. Robson (ed.), *Public Enterprise*, Allen and Unwin, 1937.
H. H. Wilson, *Pressure Group*, Secker and Warburg, 1961.

Personal Memoirs

Reginald Bevins, *The Greasy Pole*, Hodder and Stoughton, 1965.
Harman Grisewood, *One Thing At A Time*, Hutchinson, 1968.
Simon of Wythenshawe, *The BBC From Within*, Gollancz, 1953.
Charles Stuart (ed.), *The Reith Diaries*, Collins, 1975.

Discussion of Accountability and Independence

ACTT Television Commission: *One Week*, 1971.
          Report to Annual Conference 1972.
          TV4, 1971.
Charles Curran, 'The Independence of the Broadcaster', speech to The Royal Television Society, September 1975.
J. Curran, M. Gurevitch and J. C. Woollacott (eds.), *Mass Communication and Society*, Edward Arnold, 1977.
Brian Groombridge, *Television and the People*, Penguin Education Special, 1972.
Lord Hill of Luton, 'Freedom of the Communicator', BBC, April, 1968.
The People and the Media, Labour Party, 1974.
SCOB Papers: Evidence of the Standing Conference on Broadcasting submitted to the Committee on the Future of Broadcasting 1975 (available from the Acton Society Trust, 9 Poland Street, London W1).
John Scupham, *Broadcasting and the Community*, Watts, 1967.
Sir Michael Swann, *The Responsibility of the Governors*, BBC, 1974.
Mary Warnock, 'Accountability, Responsibility – or Both?', *Independent Broadcasting*, No. 2, 1974.
E. G. Wedell, *Broadcasting and Public Policy*, Michael Joseph, 1968.
Raymond Williams, *Communications*, Chatto and Windus, 1966.
—, *Television: Technology and Cultural Form*, Fontana, 1974.